M000273701

# The New Poetics

Mathew Timmons

*with an Introduction by*
*Rodrigo Toscano*

TrenchArt: Maneuvers Series

𝄢

**Les Figues Press**
Los Angeles

The New Poetics
FIRST EDITION

ISBN 13: 978-1-934254-15-8
ISBN 10: 1-934254-15-0
Library of Congress Control Number:  2010922667

Les Figues Press thanks its members for their support and readership.  Les Figues Press is a 501(c)3 organization.  Donations are tax-deductible.

This project is supported in part by generous grants from the Los Angeles County Board of Supervisors through the Los Angeles County Arts Commission and from the National Endowment of the Arts.

Les Figues would like to acknowledge the following individuals for their generosity: Johanna Blakley and Peter Binkow, Diane and Chris Calkins, and Coco Owen.  Special thanks also to Chris Hershey-Van Horn, Sylvia McNamara, Emily Kiernan, and Vincent Dachy.

The author would like to humbly thank Harold Abramowitz and Allison Carter for reading this work in manuscript form and for offering their brilliant insights. Thank you also to Matthew Klane, Lawrence Giffin and Del Ray Cross for recognizing this work by publishing pieces from the manuscript in journals and anthologies. Thank you also to my parents, Joseph and Sharon Timmons, and to my sister, Stacia Timmons, for supporting me and my work.

The New List was compiled in less than hour via Facebook by Robert Crouch, Francaise Maischic, Jeff Gaul, Deborah Russell, Steven Salardino, Ann Forrester, Janice Lee, Prayer Trairatvorakul, Jonathan Skinner, Kelly Lydick, Colin Dickey, Millicent Accardi, Myriam Moscona, Gregory Betts, Harold Abramowitz, K. Lorraine Graham, and Teresa Carmody.

Distributed by SPD / Small Press Distribution
1341 Seventh Street | Berkeley, CA  94710
www.spdbooks.org

TrenchArt 5/4
Book 5 of 5 in the TRENCHART Maneuvers Series.

**LES FIGUES PRESS**
Post Office Box 7736  |  Los Angeles, CA  90007
www.lesfigues.com

# Contents

# Introduction

Recalling Raymond Williams concepts of "dominant", "residual", and "emergent" as a concomitant (and yet discontinuous and non-contiguous) framework for understanding the complex and dynamic ways in which a culture operates, Mathew Timmons' grand mash ups of "The New" entreats the reader into an overt engagement with misrecognition of cultural locations in time & space. Since "the new" is always a negotiated, but never "settled" haggle between the Dominant & Residual & Emergent, it is perhaps the most contended-over mass popular of lived temporalities. Merely blurt "the new" and watch the popcorn fly, dare and design "the new" (order—emergent?) and keep a close eye on the Exit signs!

*The New Poetics* is not a work that is waiting to be "discovered" by analytics, rather it is a kind of analytics counter itself ("two visits today by exploited grad student tackling Burger's theory of the avant garde" "25 hits from furious non-academic historical materialist in search of "new" poetic reading apparatuses where individual word choices count for something more than select-all / paste / voila my new book", etc). So what is its "function" (as a residual positivistic inlay likes to put it)?

This book is about the partly-true edging the fully-false. Result? Reader "feels" their "individual" tolerance for culture-reading—period; that is, from not wanting to read anymore—at all, to craving a "new" glut of it. Timmons' brilliant maneuver is to employ a hyper-contiguousness of distant cultural-historical locations to eviscerate the already-tripped-up taxonomies of culture-at-large. One "result" (as a dominant mens insana in corporo caelestis internetium is wont to put it) is a husking off of social-political prefabbed fairytales. It's ok to yell "crowded" in a burning theater.

Rodrigo Toscano

New York City
2010

# The New Poetics

## The New Acrostic

From philosophy comes The New Acrostic (a fashion going back to Napoleon), in which a message is contained within the initial letters of the precious pendant. Just as the first acrostic marked the stylistic change from the narrative prologue to the more poetical preamble, The New Acrostic occurs at a transition. And I was only just figuring out what tulips stood for (I'm new to Calvinism too). I appreciate your book and DVD reviews, the inner letters of which are hidden and follow one another in their proper sequence from one visible end to the other visible end of The New Acrostic. Whoever wins the game, in my opinion, will become the next Game Master and set The New Acrostic word—an example of such poetry as required.

## The New Aesthetic

In these four lectures, we track the chronology of Beethoven's fourth, fifth, and sixth symphonies and study The New Art that had the power to revive and prolong the city's established architectural traditions. 10

From this web of paradox, The New Aesthetic has emerged.

Here, a parallel can usefully be drawn with The New Aesthetic of Bulgarian choral music represented by the various state ensembles and their repertoire of forms. Taken first from a sense of rejecting the past of modernity, The New Aesthetic encountered foreignness on the streets, a foreignness formed out of Form, taken first from a sense of rejecting the past along with modernity. The New Aesthetic encountered foreignness on the streets, a foreignness formed out of the digital aesthetics, The New Labels and The New Aesthetic. Modern photographers working in The New Aesthetic don't attempt to hide the atrocities of contemporary life.

Having considered specific art practices such as digital photography, net art, and music, we will move on to The New Aesthetic, emphasizing the potential of technology to make force more precise. Yes, War is very much related to The New Aesthetic. A glamorous and especially virtuous activity, War has taken firm hold in the American consciousness and has consolidated The New Aesthetic. A controversial exhibit was scheduled for The New Aesthetic that reinforced this heightened predilection of War for arms that have caused the appearance of The New Aesthetic in the recent years of war.

You've heard this story before, becoming unravelled in Europe or assaulted in some roadhouse, but bold as nipples and booted, The New Aesthetic is a band based out of Winnipeg. They're a hard working group who book their own tours. They've also recently recorded an EP *Desecrating Christ: The New Aesthetic of Terror?*

The New Aesthetic: did it work?

The Most popular tricks of The New Aesthetic. Minutes to Midnight. Minutes to Midnight. Not too late. Not too late for The New Aesthetic: The New Aesthetic revels in the common murky topics.

Critics and listeners raised on punk's supposed anti-hippie credo can be suspicious, while others remember the '60s.

Look Smart, Healthy and Fit in comparison with The New Aesthetic brought on by Andy Warhol. Flexible form is provided free by approaching The New Art Form, which raises questions in the very home of The New Aesthetic. The New Aesthetic formed in February of 2004 as the result of previous originals which did not work out for drummers of The New Aesthetic.

10

Notes on The New Aesthetic of poetry and music have pushed 269 of The New Readers toward The New Aesthetic. "We can hardly put too much stress on the influence which at all times the past of art exerts on the future of art, what we could call The New Aesthetic."

85

The New Aesthetic of Internet hybrids and worldwide interactive events has come from a credible source, the International Conference on Computer Graphics and Interactive Techniques of Erosion Control, a professional magazine supporting the erosion control industry, published by Forester Communications, INC. But poets still fight for the simple right to set their rhythms down on paper.

City Lofts. City Lofts. City Lofts. City Lofts. This neighborhood plans tours and projects status. The New Aesthetic supports carriers of One Edge Now! Minutes To Midnight. Minutes To Midnight. The most popular tricks.

Besides reflecting on the conditions that made possible this recent boom, this book elaborates on The New Aesthetic and the tendencies of recent productions. This is a polemic against both, and distinctly agrees with Schiller that critics of The New Aesthetic misunderstand the idea of beauty when they say, "The New Aesthetic is not everyone's cup of herbal tea."

As Guattari acknowledges, The New Aesthetic is a paradigm consonant with Marcel Duchamp's observation many years ago that "art is a road which leads."

## The New Aesthetic Statement

With the clarifying role of *Self-Portrait with Easel* (1888), we may clearly recognize The New Aesthetic Statement underlying the whole series.

## The New Affect

## The New Alexandrine

In Marx's view, Capitalism opened up a space for global socialism, so that The New Alexandrine could offer us the chance to embrace ideas of progress. However, there were some countries, such as Phoenicia, where the Attic Standard had never taken firm root in The New Alexandrine. As wielded by

Hugo, The New Alexandrine would accept none of the artificial constraints imposed, rhetorical or prosodic, and has taken part in international projects of great stature. Founded originally by Cleopatra, The New Alexandrine was a copy of the later version revised by some person well skilled in the Hebrew language, and was deposited in The New Library of The New    50 Alexandrine. After the symbolic layering of numerous works, most bookhouses use the volumes therein for manuscripts written within The New Alexandrine.

The New Alexandrine is situated in front of the compound Library of Social and Human Science Faculties in Shatby. We will see the Roman remains including Pompey's Column made by pink granite from Aswan, a foundation for The New Alexandrine, inaugurated in October 2002. A major part of its façade overlooks The New Library of Alexandria    50 and The New Alexandrine. The construction of the library at Alexandria, Egypt, is The New Alexandrine. Covering an area of 70,000 square meters, the library is nearing completion.

The New Horizons is the Foundation being set up    42 with considerable objectives and a modest budget of some $11 million dollars. Their headquarters are located firmly within The New Myth—The New    61 Hypertext Library will be a reality in an age designed    42 for technology and The New Alexandrine. The entire Alexandria Travel Guide Library is a virtual Bibliotheca of The New Alexandrine. The New Alexandrine in Hypertext and Reality: A Technology for the Age of Myth.

The Library, see my Journal Library, the Library is a Library Guide sent by the Library, a technology fit for the Age of The New Alexandrine.

Quell'incunabolo è già un ipertesto—that incunable is already a hypertext. Not to mention the gosh-wow revelation of a map you can find in any ancient atlas, and all the silly people trekking with great drama into The New Alexandrine.

I totally missed this last week, but here's some news on the development of The New Alexandrine located in a place between the Virtual Library, the Bibliotheca Alexandrina and The New Alexandrine. The first of several new businesses to come to The New Alexandrine in southeast Shreveport is a place called the Library n' Home Design Center and more.

**The New Approach to Nature**

This is November 13, 2006, and there are instruments and ways of forming reality that are similar, if not identical, to those requested by digital technologies and The New Approach to Nature. On the other hand, nanotechnology can be seen as the outcome of The New Approach to Nature initiated and developed by Materials Science and Engineering. Jeremy Rifkin, in his popular book, *The Biotech Century* (1998: 67-72), underlines this dichotomy and goes so far as to attempt a definition of The New Approach to Nature. His paper focuses on the analysis of the bio-centric attitude, which is an example of The New Approach to Nature and of man's position in Nature.

The government has announced The New Approach to Nature in a recently released white paper, The Government Communication on The New Approach to Nature. Although responsibility for water management does not currently rest with the many, The New Approach to Nature acts as a stand in for the many as it is ascribed all the attributes of a legitimate consumer of water. The New Approach to Nature also turns out to be an old one, that of celebrating fertility and conservation in the implementation of protected areas. The New Approach to Nature was applied to make possible an ever-illuminating glimpse of the mutual relationships of those people who carried it out.

Writers and thinkers, reflect on this work of literature for the masses, The New Approach to Nature, origin, native language, custom, and community.

Brecht feels that The New Approach to Nature "was not applied to society" (184). The New Approach to Nature was not applied to society. He advocates for The New Science of Society, in which people who are  89
not content with The New Approach to Nature could take solace in its emphasis on a scientific analysis of its models, and sidestep sentimentality.

Another phase of The New Approach to Nature can be seen in a painting attributed to Chao Meng-fu from the Yuan period now on display at the Freer Gallery of Art. At that time, the changes in the visual arts were treated as if they illustrated continuity and the role of the arts in The New Approach to Nature, as well as showing the cohesiveness of The New Theory of Colour.  102

108 Two great poets of the Romantic movement made possible The New Approach to Nature characterized by The New Writing collected in the volume, *Lyrical Ballads, with a Few Other Poems* by William Wordsworth and Samuel Taylor Coleridge, published in 1798.

**The New Art**

**The New Art Form**

**The New Ashes**

**The New Author Function**

And in the hopes of a larger and increasingly literate audience paradoxically inseparable from The New Author Function and from reception, elements of The New Author Function in narrative seem quite incompatible with tradition.

The New Author Function constitutes itself as figuring forth. Is it The New Author Function making itself felt, or the mark of a re-appraisal of Horatian modality throughout, which, ironically, the images (and illusions) of procreation actually obscure?

Is this the presumed autonomy of The New Author Function as presupposed? The connotation that the Author brings to the text is often less than helpful for innovative writing, yet it is making The New Author Function.

Creating an Author creates The New Record in the Authors' table and returns the ID assigned to The New Author Function.

86

Create an Author. Create an Author Name. Create a String as String and the two as a String are.

**The New Authority**

**The New Baby**

**The New Birds**

Given my apparent fascination with bird brains, and their evident ability to functionally imitate mammalian brains, The New Birds have become my little navigation tools after doing a lot of work on their Eyes. In Vermont, I was asked to write a little about this project for Stephen, I wrote—a little Love equals The New Birds—Thank you, thank you, thank you!!! Not only was this a lot of fun to write, but it seemed to get a lot of response from people. I always make sure no one is getting hurt and that The New Birds are allowed access to food and water by placing food and water in multiple places and, during my free time, by writing an interesting article on enabling The New Birds.

The New Birds and Bees use and care for your flock of messages first, then care for The New Birds, watching The New Birds closely for signs of disease before putting them down in your detailed surveys which tell how many pairs of Malleefowl there are among The New Birds. You basically totally isolate The New Birds from the old birds, only deal with The New Birds after you're done taking care of the old flock.

I stumbled upon this site quite a few months back and wondered, if The New Birds to be introduced are younger than the existing flock, should I do the usual and get the enclosure as dark as possible before introducing The New Birds? Two of The New Birds came from the Oregon Zoo, another two from the Philadelphia Zoo and a single bird from Sea World. This species of penguins likes "Naming" The New Birds.

Where are we with The New Birds?

The New Birds are quite a bit larger with heavier bills and tails at least twice as big as a brewer's. The finsterium light went out at 8:13 p.m., which of course startled all The New Birds and then it took five hours for them to join the rest of the birds, but the team waited diligently, watching the pecking order change as The New Birds approached the veterans.

Based on average densities, The New Birds of the West Midlands cover all of Staffordshire, Warwickshire,

Worcestershire, and the former West Midlands County. The New Birds aren't fitted with satellite tracking devices, but are eager to track The New Birds if funding allows. Voila! The New Birds are part of a multimillion-dollar investment in growth. A local resident of the West will christen The New Blood 16 by setting up The New Birds of Prey as a formidable espionage unit with a burgeoning roster of super-heroine specialists.

When I was everybody I often asked myself, Hello, how come, hey…

The New Birds are birds and The New Birds could be described as a new species within the species of ancestral short-legged shore birds, there is a range of leg, and I look forward to hearing about The New Birds you see. Use your word, pass on your name, and get to know The New Birds on the Bay, their current color and their issues.

Where are we with The New Birds?

Once, on the Bay, the Dock of the Bay, Ms. Scanlon said she was all navigation—Eye by Eye line—ever since she bought the original Eye. The New Birds, their eyes, the navigation. After buying the pair from a person that does regular vet checks and blood tests, the woman felt confident that The New Birds were healthy.

Fish are The New Birds! A Great update for the Eye interface, fixing the traffic map bug!

The New Birds of Prey Go Back to Paw Talk in the Pet Forums to have Bird Discussions with Other Pets.

One week later—and hello! Alu! Remember me? and The New Birds!?

What do you think of The New Birds?

The tourists can simply put The New Birds back into their cocoons or lash themselves to The New Birds and get out of the way. "We firmly believe that managing carbohydrate intake will send The New Birds up and up until they are mere specks in the sky."

**The New Blank Verse**

In more places than one, "rude beggarly riming" has been denounced not (as might have been done with some colour) in favour of The New Blank Verse, but actually as the sole dramatic vehicle, adopted in place of The New Blank Verse which Surrey had used for his translation of the *Aeneid*, and which made him seem a marvelous poet, the man who first demonstrated that powerful dramatic poetry could be written in The New Blank Verse.

Every loft in Cheapside published its Magnum Folium (or magazine) of The New Blank Verse. The Cheapside Players would produce anything on sight as long as the lineup stretched toward drama and seemed in alignment with those virginal, foresworn invisibles for whom pink is The New Blank Verse (appearances can be discerning—what wheels against The New Blank Verse).

So, perhaps more than anything else, free verse is sometimes confused with The New Blank Verse, which does not rhyme but has a set metrical pattern. Prose and The New Blank Verse work in the interest of a literal acting style, one in which the action unequivocally underscores the message of the text. Free verse, on the other hand, takes up The New Blank Verse from the lips of Surrey, and turns it to its right use of tragedy. We cannot say that he does for it what pink does for The New Blank Verse (appearances can be discerning—what wheels these henpecked butter huts do to the will).

As for Shakespeare, he has sometimes been conjecturally associated with The Queen's Men, his King John, and King Lear. And it's just; it was Lord Dorset and Sackville over whom Marlowe had twice triumphed on the London stage, particularly with Tamburlaine, championing and refining The New Blank Verse.

Many believe that if he had lived and the fluctuating rhythms that had once nervously charted a chord or even a change of mood were to return again, supported by the framework of The New Blank Verse, the most characteristic form of Elizabethan music would therefore have coincided with The New Blank Verse, the dramas and the sonnet sequences, along with the great outburst of the imitation of non-University scribblers (whether as imitators of The New Blank Verse, or as "translators" of Seneca and the Italians).

Every loft in Cheapside publishes its Magnum Folium (or magazine) of The New Blank Verse. The Cheapside Players will produce anything on sight as long as it discards the rhymed meter which has hitherto been the sole dramatic vehicle, and adopts in its place The New Blank Verse which Surrey had used.

In this sample of The New Blank Verse, based on the stress-rhythm theory from the mountain of the gods, the unappeasable gods, are such lines metrical? These words seem to express the apprehensions of a jealous rival who warns his associates that Shakespeare has copied The New Blank Verse which every loft in Cheapside publishes in its Magnum Folium (or magazine) of The New Blank Verse. The Cheapside Players would produce anything on sight as long as it had style.

**The New Blood**

**The New Body**

**The New Bones**

**The New Books**

**The New Boring**

**The New Box**

**The New Caesura**

I consider this proclivity on Nietzsche's part to claim himself as The New Caesura of time and history to display a complete lack of sobriety and alongside his belief that he had become The New Caesura, the destiny, the great divide of history, it can be ascribed to his "jealousy of Jesus." (Nietzsche, for what it's worth, The New Caesura looks exactly right to me.) Thanks dude, are you coming to the show in Vermont? (I didn't understand the previous symbol for caesura; I have certainly, finally understood, I believe, that some people are still waiting for The New Caesura glyph. Sorry for the delay, I will submit to it soon.) So, you like The New Caesura? Shit, it's so Damn Amazing. But to some, The New Caesura is just alright, just another version of the old connect–i–cut.

**The New Cars**

**The New Challenge**

**The New Chapters**

## The New Christianity

### The New Church

18    The New Christianity is based on the Old Testaments and the Writings of Emanuel. The New Church, on the other hand, is founded on the belief that the Lord God can be seen as an overview of what The New Church teaches about Life After Death. The New Church is a common name for a religious movement based on the teachings found in the works written by a college of the liberal arts dedicated to comprehensive instruction in the arts and sciences in light of the teachings of The New Church. This will introduce you

108    to The New Way of Life. Perhaps you are not satisfied with your present one? Your gateway to accessing comprehensive resources about The New Church is

60    part of The New Movements.

What is new about The New Church? Please contact us if you have any questions or join us on Sunday morning at 9:30 a.m. with candles, bring two or more. We are creating The New Church for people in the 21st Century. Home is The New Church. The Lords of The New Church Live For Today! What do we offer besides Rare Memorabilia? A seminary providing instruction in The New Church doctrine. Dance with us, Lords of The New Church! Hello Dr. Faustus, you have either turned off The New Church or you are stuck in an old version. At the Grand Opening of The New Church in New York on September 25th, 2004, the keynote speech presented the first of the "A" texts explaining that The Lords of

The New Church are a punk rock supergroup. The New Church is made of Materials, of Sections, of Music, of The Lords of The New Church.

The New Church has existed as a congregation in New York City of spiritual and religious movements related to The New Church. Based on theological writings, The New Church has branches all over the world, but the one located in this area believes that The New Church is 30 volumes of writings marked as the second *Discover For Yourself Why* series. This little known, but much loved, 250 year-old church provides parishioners of all races in all countries a deeper and totally General Church of The New. Those who accept The New Church seek to realize The New Church spoken of in the presence of the Lord of The New Church. The New Church teaches us to look past the institution consisting of independently operating schools that provide high quality education enhanced by the doctrine of The New Church. After a moving ceremony featuring speeches from executives and leading human rights advocates, the President of The New Church presented The Method of Our Madness to the Lords of The New Church and The Angels in Exile organisation. The New Church is founded on the belief that the Lord God Jesus Christ is The Writings of The New Church, telling of the infinite love of God and helping us to know Who We Are, What We Believe, and What Is The New Church. The New Church is The Heavenly Doctrine and the Blessed Sacrament of text, text, text, text, text, text, text, text, text.

**The New Clothes**

## The New Collapse

Let us anticipate the publication of The New Collapse with a collapse of philosophy and research. The New Collapse will curve the surface of operations.

At left, the aerial view taken in July shows two spatter cones of the The New Collapse, and once the equation is standardized by API and ISO, it will provide additional performance and safety factors
50 for designing The New Collapse. The New Level is quite close to optimal: there is an oracle relative to which NP is contained in P/poly but the aerial view taken on October 13 shows The New Collapse, a pit in the West Gap. If the current rates of renewed
42 growth are maintained then The New Hexagon will fill The New Collapse within a few months and this large depression dome will lead an exclusive guided, adventure tour of The New Collapse.

Buy tickets if you want, or get on the Guestbook
51 for some cool comps—you can buy The New Links online: 6:30 tour (SOLD OUT), 7:30 tour (SOLD OUT), 8:30 tour (SOLD OUT).

Wouldn't it be great if you could select The New Collapse?

Under the broad cause of lost form, a definition of The New Collapse applies to collapse from under the weight of people or personal property or the weight of a rain check for The New Collapse. However, in The New Collapse simulator we've added new variables to avoid this problem. Also, in the old simulator, randomness was used to fabricate difference, a sign of The New Collapse to come.

The New Collapse button is good, but it would be more obvious for that functionality to be implemented when the user presses the Close button on the search. In the meantime, The New Collapse test unit has been put to successful use a number of times and therefore represents a highly expedient expansion of the Surface Collapse Test.

The New Collapse is a virtual surface command operation that curves and surfaces collapse.

The activity subsequent to the collapse in the northern shield was preferentially concentrated in the interior basin of The New Collapse, quickly building a comparison of The New Collapse to some classical pre-main-sequence hydrostatic tracks, showing that D-burning ignites and mostly occurs during the The New Collapse. The New Collapse function #3 is in excellent agreement with The New Numerical Evaluations. This is shown in Fig. 1 for n=25 70 photons. Loving The New Collapse? It makes the entire landscape scroll across your thumbnail, even if just to see one picture.

A comparison of The New Collapse and the pre-main sequence tracks to classical hydrostatic tracks shows that: (1) The New Collapse ages full time (2) it's just a glitch with the way animation is being read? Anyway,

(3) head over to the files section to pick up The New Collapse and it's map rendering code!

The pit after a creative lull is reminiscent of the "Great Pit," which formed on the west slope of the cone in early 1993, and enlarged until the west wall went:

XxxxxxxxxxxxxxxxxxxxxxxxxxxxxxxxxxxxxxxxxxxxxxxxxxxX.

The Contractors have made frantic attempts to cover up and deny The New Collapse.

Then, The New Collapse clicked in and brought back that blue macro to the way it was before, expanding some and recording 11 attacks that rattled the area and sent some rescue workers from ground zero racing towards The New Collapse in a search for survivors. The first collapse sent the Ants Scrambling starting on January 29. At the time of the collapse, we were out on Church Street and came away from flying debris, concrete and smoke as ambulances began to scream from all directions, responding to The New Collapse.

26    Contact the champion! The New Cone Crazy Champion is champion! The Collapse of Heaven and Earth, The Collapse Of The Fourth World. The New Collapse!!! AAAaaaaaaahhhhhHHHHHHHH!!!! Click Me, Feel Me. This Is Going To Be One Insane Show Filled With Bad Vibes. HeHeHe! LIVE!!!!!!

58    However, The New Motherfuckers are keeping their Clutch Secret from El Cid, Chief… to exhibit their Heels within the main dome of The New Collapse. The delay between the supernova explosion generating

the metastable neutron star and The New Collapse can explain the delay proposed for The Troubadour.

## The New Color

## The New Community

## The New Company

## The New Concept

Automatically see The New Concept!

In this paper, I will address The New Concept of equality in European community law. I will do this by distinguishing between four different meanings of equality outlined by The New Concept for transport and city planning in the EU. There is a Type and Policy of The New Concept: a) Country b) Western Europe c) Austria d) Language.

The New Concept is striking out with repeated admissions of national weakness. Operationalizing The New Concept of sexual and reproductive health in Indonesia is like The New Politics of family planning in the 1990s. Some analysts of The New Concept have attributed the confrontational posture exhibited on various websites dealing with The New Concept, to the stated fact that sightings of The New Concept can be attributed to many different things. The Gulf War has significantly influenced our attitudes and perceptions about war, for example. The New Concept views war as conflict won quickly and decisively. The New Concept in Nicaragua can easily be seen in the Art and Popular Culture of the contemporary era since the Revolution in 1979, most principally after the Iran-Contra affair of the mid 80s.

The New Concept of periodontal disease pathogenesis requires new and novel therapeutic strategies as I have argued in the *Journal of Clinical Periodontology* (34 (5), 367–369). There you may find technical specifications, photos and a history of The New Concept. You may also get the latest news and announcements from Chevy on the 2009 Chevy Camaro car. The Inside Line: It's bigger than a bread box and also looks a bit like one, plus it comes with a "perfume diffuser."

A typical concept? The need exists to improve The New Concept.

The New Concept of Universal Service is a Digital Networked Communications Environment. Blogosthing's reaction to The New Concept of BlogTV! in Colombia offers a small portrait of the author, Blogosthing, in Colombia, as he reacts to The New Concept of BlogTV! As we have already mentioned, the telecommunications sector at Samsung has called The New Concept an "experience store," despite fears from the shopping center's owners that it would become a costly nap room for The New Concept.

It's impossible to design for fast Fourth of July-volume traffic, so the least we can do is offer motorists a pleasant view of things, not just more asphalt.

Picture In a Picture: The New Concept is embodied in Cars displayed at this year's Carlisle All-Ford Nationals, June 4-6. Ford's newest study is called Fordiosis Auto X! and it's a successor to last year's iosis. The New Concept is like a car in the future—an indication of The New Concept.

It isn't clear whether or not The New Concept restaurant will be ready for a fall debut, but diners won't have a lack of places to eat in the meantime. "How would you prove the forwardness of The New Concept today?" That's the question the November 24 issue of *Caijing* magazine asks. To even understand the question, you need to know this: who are generally the intended end-users of The New Concept?

*Latin Characterizations of Scattering Functions: An Analytical Essay and Compendium of Illustrations* came out of The New Concept of complex multi-fractal stages. The New Concept has stimulated a gallery full of Illustrations of The New Concept. The presence of these illustrations, drawn by the chief designer of *Silver Shooting Stars and the Japanese Page*, filed under The New Concept of HyperBase Experimentation, shows the various projects of the First Emperor of China.

It would be wrong to tie the reality of The New Concept to an idea of The New Concept right from the start. These past months we've received a lot of suggestions with ideas and proposals for The New Concept. We even created new photo albums for The New Image and opened various threads regarding this. For employers, confidence in The New Concept would bring the promise of improved human resources with transatlantic qualifications.

I believe that starting companies is more fun and profitable than any other human endeavor, and to streamline the process of manufacturing The New Concept, I have built a factory.

**The New Concrete Poem**

... Related words: Concrete.

Finally The New Concrete Poem, with stretched word, pounded and swooned and reshaped lines.

Splattered with color and colored like a coloring book, extended.

Finally The New Concrete Poem, with stretched word, pounded and swooned and reshaped lines.

**The New Cone Crazy Champion**

**The New Craft**

**The New Criticism**

**The New Cultural Productivity**

**The New Culture**

**The New Dawn**

**The New Day**

**The New Deal**

**The New Death**

**The New Debility**

Hendrix was in England for two weeks before coming home. He remains unresolved about The New Debility and debates the amount of continued advertising being devoted to the war against Bolshevism. However, everything has gone brilliantly and after this type of surgical operation one comes to accept The New Debility. All property owners want heat and insurance, and will eventually recognize the contributions made by The New Debility.

for Will Alexander

## The New Different

## The New Difficult

## The New Dirty

## The New Disposition

I have heard from many individuals in the community about several concerns relating to the process for developing the standards and content of The New Disposition.

1. Press the [Add Code] key to accept The New Disposition.

2. Enter The New Disposition and date.

3. The Old World, the continental, and the revocation of the bequest in the will should not be operative unless The New Disposition of the subject of the bequest should prove effectual. In the case where the assumed revocation is previous to The New Disposition, it can be intended to pave the way for revocation.

4. See, instead, "TEST 2."

5. Hearing is not expressly made conditional on the subsistence of The New Disposition, but the same effect follows, the revocation is effectual and the heir will ensure that The New Disposition is adequately funded in this area so that the gridded structure of The New Disposition is successfully implemented.

6. Press the [Add Code] key, and add The New Disposition.

7. Enter The New Disposition of code.

8. Complete The New Disposition to program the CM DS C3 screen as described above. You can only enter the Direct Sale field if the asset follows the method of The New Disposition. At the currently planned maximum core loading of 40% max, in fact, DOE may need even more than two reactors to carry out The New Disposition. Enter The New Disposition only in regards to the rate that we may not maintain, while on the other hand, emphasizing the positive side of The New Disposition. A successful call of geists that specifies The New Disposition as oldish should return the previous disposition of the signal.

In reference to the Acquisition and Disposition of the Atlantic Ocean, begin with a Contrast between the Old World, The New Disposition and its continental mass. The Old World is continental while The New Disposition includes a conversion by believers that leads them to actively unite in a union involving ontological participation.

Having established this point, Kant takes the remarkable step of asserting that The New Disposition "takes the place" (*vertritt*) of the old. But the Holy Spirit is the one who makes these irreconcilable opposites, the old disposition and The New Disposition, understandable. The Version Type specifies which Type is to be attributed to the faulty copy, while The New Disposition specifies The New Disposition to be assigned to the faulty copy.

In an earlier book, *In the Days of the Comet*, The New Disposition was the result of the Great Change. Here, though engaged in no brilliant action, The New Disposition references the characteristic of the restriction level vis-a-vis the needs of a child. During The New Disposition of the army in 1781, General Wayne's division was thrown into the southern army. Since the resignation of Mr. Clark there have been various rumors to the effect that the New York Central Park owners would take a hand in The New Disposition to retain possession of the ball and that the offense would find new plays, which would openly conform to The New Disposition of the players on the field.

This effectual calling finally secures, through the truth as means, the first holy exercise of The New Disposition that is born in the soul of the Atlantic Ocean—Contrast the Old World to The New Disposition of continental masses and its consequences. The New Disposition is with the same propriety styled disinterestedness; attachment; love; good-will; benevolence; and the spirit, inclining the one in whom it exists to see to it that once the case goes to trial or a guilty plea is entered, The New Disposition and sentence should be recorded appropriately as The New Disposition, finally.

The call to repentance aims at a confession of sin and a new moral life. The policy of The New Disposition presents numerous options for the disposition of records and encourages the identification of other bodies to take the record as truth. Of The New Disposition, which may be to increase the disposition in the residuary clause, it can be said that The New Disposition is being made under authority of the state. The New Disposition is, with the same propriety, styled disinterestedness; love; goodwill; benevolence; and the spirit inclining the one in whom it exists to think this a very probable condition.

## The New Distance

## The New Doe

## The New Earth

## The New Echo

## The New Economy

**The New Edition**

**The New Effect**

**The New Ego**

**The New Egret**

The development of The New Egret took place in a field in early 2002. A 22 million dollar contract was awarded to Technip-CoFlexip for research and development. The minimum build requirements of The New Egret included 4,000 sq. ft. of air, using one of the preferred builders from Earth: Palmira Member No. 241.

The expected fluxes in the first Z-burst model were chosen for optimal parameters together with limits for free fluxes in The New Egret limit. Our numbers indicate an estimate of the cosmic ray data, as in Figure 1, whereas The New Egret flux is shown only as an external function, as an option within The New Package. We've made use of The New Egret to generate data published since our last paper. Our analysis now indicates that the massive black hole we hypothesized will probably not come from an infraction of The New Egret. The numbers indicate only a fraction of The New Egret. More significantly, when comparing The New Egret to the inner Galaxy above, the spectrum is much too difficult.

The shape of the curve between redshifts is mainly determined by the evolution index.

Our members have identified The New Egret as Phase-Averaged Emission derived from the photon spectrum. The numbers only indicate a fraction of The New Egret, an estimate of the extragalactic diffusion. As seen from Fig. 9, The New Egret position is well within the error box and is consistent with its position. In this manner, The New Egret hinders the photonflux in a severely limited region and has contributed to the decay of X-particles.

Also, note The New Egret just across the river. We are tracking activity at thirty nests, and have used our data to form The New Egret.

The New Egret strongly disfavours extragalactic boundaries, thus top-down fluxes limit the various upper neutrinos instead of The New Egret limit. Here, The New Egret limit is lower than the set of errors easiest to see in the maps of The New Egret. In several energy ranges, the high-resolution figures are gouped together with various limits of neutrino fluxes—also note The New Egret limit.

With The New Egret as a trailblazer, we made a logo for T-shirts as supplies allowed. The New Egret, of course beautifully complements the Ibis and Osprey, and is designed to ensure they flow together seamlessly.

An abstract catalog on "grazars" (blazers which are observed to be high-energy gamma-ray sources) has brought together gamma-ray emissions from directions that are modulated by the Cen X-3 pulsar spin period, all leading us to identify The New Egret as the source. The New Egret observations have not yet been successfully exploited to discriminate among the various proposed models without violating The New Egret bounds.

Similiar to the case of the Z-burst model, The New Egret will be The New Emotion once it is given to us as such. Windows for Windows.

Many of the bounds derived here were found using The New Egret which allowed us to look at higher energy G-rays, furthermore, our analysis of groups and the community of airplanes, boats and cars, has encountered two problems. Extrapolating from what we've been told about The New Egret, we're able to come to two conflicting conclusions 1. It Sucks and 2. Compared to say, Astro City, The New Egret is sweet.

The angle of The New Egret monitor is odd and getting all ready for the sway of this weird, sweet boat. By the way, if we could afford another boat, we'd buy one in a second, especially if it overlooked the fair 9th course of The New Egret.

The New Egret is a tsunami along with The New Tsuba we ordered from Bugei. We could not get the tsuka to fit back perfect so we had to shave the menugi bamboo neutrinos. If you're in NC and take a tour of The New Egret facility, afterwards you might be tempted to say the perfectly apt phrase, "Hint hint."

for Vanessa Place

## The New Elegiac

By the last ten or fifteen years of the sixteenth century, the time at which The New Elegiac couplet burst into English poetry, the English heroic passed into The New Elegiac. In fact, none of The New Elegiac can be assigned definitively to a separate poem of either battle. It can be shown, however, that the evidence *Die Brautwahl*, when it was first performed in 1912, proved to be an orchestral *embarras de richesse* with elements of The New Elegiac, a style gracing and in keeping with the poetic project of diversification.

This is a that.

The New Elegiac, in addition to being linguistic, is a configuration of Shelley's re-enacting and re-writing the story of his subject. Keats, also proposes to host "a bag of ash" which indirectly reflects The New Elegiac in a sense of continuing responsibility to the dead. Deianira knows very well, just as she clearly knows the opening distich of her very own letter, written in The New Elegiac, a work of verse in three parts: The first two parts contain advice for the predatory male, and the third devotes itself to the opposite sex. When that eclogue became long enough for two, she switched calendars and made The New Elegiac, pairing November and December, then wrote or adapted The New February.

39

The New Elegiac has gone on to form novel fragments in Canada and to compose a keynote address. But more significant in our appreciation of Propertius' expansion of the range of possible meanings of arms in The New Elegiac is the world of cities and books

Simonides and his Thessalian clients traffic and somewhat miss. Grief insists, like naming, carries sexual connotations, and has again, in The New Elegiac, become a world.

This mediating function places The New Elegiac between the real fighter Ovid, even in his old age, and the theme of the poet grown old embodied in the prince, a position devoted entirely to The New Elegiac and the fragments of Simonides, but in a ritual act that appeared too late to be taken into account here.

We now know, from The New Elegiac, that Theocritus looked back to the Plataea poem:

He quoted fragments to us.

## The New Emotion

The New Emotion is a collection of movement: Automatic Mechanical Self-Winding Movement. The key concept of The New Emotion is a multimodal presentation by a lifelike agent of emotion expression. The computing industry of the 1990s enabled significantly higher image quality, boosting diagnostic accuracy with less radiation exposure, giving us The New Emotion. Both formats were sanctioned by the child-rearing theories of the day in which the father was admired for displaying The New Emotion while still remaining a function of The New Emotion.

Medea and The New Emotion she feels towards Creuse—an emotion which she senses is imposed on her by fate—generates her weakness and indecision, leading her into The New Emotion, turning the tables on satisfaction and toning her arms for smartness. Tables possess all of The New Emotion, turning the tables by delivering a package of satisfaction. The New Emotion is studded with 21 jewels and is of the 42-hours-of-power caliber.

According to scientists, they have yielded discoveries that are widely acknowledged as important. The field has largely welcomed The New Emotion. The beta testers are unanimous: The New Emotion feature adding sound to the available set of expressions is the best thing that has happened in a long time. Purchase The New Emotion and turn the tables on Satisfaction.

Pricing for The New Emotion will have the same recommended list/enduser price as the current innovative products that create powerful and effective branding programs for meeting the challenges and opportunities of The New Emotion-based economy. Some multimodal presentation contents are produced in The New Version to show the effectiveness of 104 The New Emotion function. The series will initially consist of three products: dynamic, heart-shaped instruments of The New Emotion. The New Emotion represents the ideal package for Dependent Individual Clients (DICs). It offers full functionality at the high-end, including such advanced versions that show the effectiveness of The New Emotion expression function.

The New Emotion has something for every taste.

In case you do not like The New Emotion, with toned arms and direct wired with the Smart Cable and Clever Clamp Combo, with a Clear Audio Aurora & Classic Variable Content, you can switch back, which will clearly show you the effectiveness of The New Emotion expression function.

Featuring Varimotion technology, The New Emotion series, taken together with The New Emotion dynamics, provides all the possibilities available. Once a Mood Algorithm is determined for The New Emotion two separate steps occur: firstly, the Learning Process, and the second consists of an Introduction to the Mood Algorithm Database.

This is the motto for The New Emotion: An interface is a necessary part of human-computer interaction. 104 The New Version will show the effectiveness of The New Emotion function. Once a Mood Algorithm is determined for The New Emotion, two separate algorithms access the Database now updated to include support of The New Emotion.

Figure 1 shows the performance of musical individuals compared to the control groups of existing tests plus the results of The New Emotion test. If the customer becomes upset during the course of the call, his speech 74 will change, and The New Pattern receives a different score for The New Emotion.

I do not expect it, The New Emotion, in spite of my training. I'll fail The New Emotion again, but I look for it now for a different reason.

**The New Enjambment**

Ride the Lightning between two brackets. Schrödinger's pangram killed his cat.

Plug in Men for the value of X, keep *The Rum Diary* nearby and use the right number sets to avoid sloppy seconds.

Welcome to The Days of The New Enjambment: A Play.


**The New Era**


**The New Ethnicities**


**The New Experiment**


**The New Fashion**


**The New Fear**


**The New February**

**The New Figure**

**The New Finance**

**The New Fire**

**The New First Kiss**

The trials of The New First Kiss included a series of formula red mixtures and entries in the form of Merlot and Tutti Fruiti mixes and Victory! The New First Kiss is like dice on a thread. Since the other one went to hell (ha ha! I made a funny!), here's another one, The New First Kisss.

No longer Juliet, nor the same author of the original, The New First Kiss has been seen and heard at least 289 times. I quote, "And doll, don't wear it out." Come check out The New First Kiss inside the love doctor, then you can listen to The New First Kiss soundtrack over and over again in New York City, Dresden and Mexico.

**The New First Kisss**

**The New Flat**

**The New Form**

**The New Format**

**The New Free Verse**

**The New Fuck**

**The New Fuckin' Song**

**The New Function**

**The New Future**

**The New Gender**

**The New Generation**

**The New Government**

**The New Hexagon**

**The New History**

**The New Horizons**

**The New Husband**

**The New Hypertext Library**

**The New I**

In the St. Louis metropolitan area, The New I will be introduced with new features and improved performance. The New I does not require The New I. Features introduced in the design of The New I will be heavily influenced by the capabilities of a wide variety

Our first topic, is actually part of a larger set of changes going under the name of The New I. This lesson will mostly talk about The New I package, detailing all the features of The New I currently in place. According to representatives from the Ocean, representatives from the Sun and representatives from the Channel, in their presentation entitled The New I Lives, The New I will lead development efforts with questions, exercises and summaries.

Now that we've reviewed the classic approach, let's look at how The New I will work abstractly to solve the problems we've seen with The New I. The editors of The New I have discussed the relaunch of The New I and The New Format as well as its focus, reducing objectionable content. What should parents do about The New I? Watch those ads! and talk to their kids about those negative ads. Perhaps the best indication of the sorry state of journalism these days is the acceptance of The New I.

There's The New I (or is it Old?) that looks to create an approach to the world of The New I niche, which will feature connectivity, news and information. Work is The New I solution of choice. What does this mean? This year new systems are arriving with more information on The New I and the motivation behind it. Check this out: The New I is completely customisable by you!!! How do you do this? Just click Replay. In the case of name changes, The New I must be made to reflect the name change and the The New I should inform the I-Center of the address to which The New I wishes to be addressed.

Central highlights of The New I project include: the rebuilding and upgrading of all bridges, interchanges, and memory interfaces in St. Louis County. The blackout during the summer of 2003 proved that the critical infrastructure of The New I, e.g., the power grid, is vulnerable. The New I will launch The New I series with The New Series analysers, name analysers, and The New Function analysers for use in the ambient world. Use of The New I is the best present that can be offered, and the most advantages can be located in character-set support. The New I says, "Look at my record." The New I does not answer wild hypotheticals.

According to experts in the Department of The New I, you must first fill out a Request Form. Attach this form to the top of the documents required for issuance of The New I. It will take a minimum of five days after all for the Future Hardware of The New I to arrive. Then, we'll put The New I shield in place. First we will orient it as shown... Thus, The New I shield must be installed so that the two big holes in the areas of buffer management and scalable network capabilities correspond to The New I improvements made by the Missouri Department of Transportation.

**The New Icon**

**The New Id**

**The New Idea**

**The New Ideal**

**The New Ideal Reading Experience**

There is no match for...

The New Ideal Reading Experience.

**The New Idiom**

**The New Image**

**The New Imperialism**

**The New Inauguration**

**The New Incentive**

**The New Independence**

**The New Innovation**

**The New Interesting**

**The New IQ**

**The New Items**

**The New Jerk**

**The New Jerusalem**

## The New Kitten

Tips related to feeding, grooming, discipline, and health care for The New Kitten! or cat.

After Mama Bear gets The New Kitten all cleaned up, the Bear family is ready to adopt her—as long as Little Lady, the puppy, doesn't mind! We want to make the introduction between The New Kitten and Brandi as friendly and painless as possible. When bringing a kitten into a home with other cats, an easy trick is to take a blanket and rub it all over your cat and then rub it all over The New Kitten. It allows your other pets to begin to get used to The New Smell of The New Kitten.

95

Welcoming The New Kitten?

Well, we have The New Kitten. His name is Jack and he's been with us about two weeks. O my God, is this cat cute. And Lacey adores him. She loves lolcats and funny pictures. Like this one of two dogs playing with The New Kitten.

We decree thee "question cat!"

Before you bring your kitten home, there are decisions to be made, especially if the kitten hasn't had all his/her shots yet. You can place The New Kitten in one room and allow the resident animal(s) to meet it, or you can hold The New Kitten on your lap and let your other cats meet it.

Remember that people (especially men) who are used to having dogs (not cats) may tend to play a little aggressively with The New Kitten. The best thing to do is to ignore the ruckus and leave them to work it out on their own. It will take a while and meanwhile, the worst thing you can do is force the situation.

Welcoming The New Kitten.

Provide a separate place for feeding The New Kitten. In time, she will be able to dine with the others, but do not force The New Kitten to compete for food. Your breeder should review with you what food The New Kitten has been eating.

At first, it would be best to have a separate room for The New Kitten. Keep The New Kitten in a different room, if possible with its own kitten food and litter. Set up the bathroom or laundry for the first few days as The New Kitten's bedroom. Place The New Kitten in a playpen or room all on its own. She will have to be confined until she learns the lay out of the house.

Put The New Kitten or cat in a room of its own and allow your new pet and the established cat to sniff at one another from under the door for a few days. Your other pets will sniff around the door of the room housing The New Kitten's lair.

Welcoming The New Kitten!

How to encourage The New Kitten and adult cats to get along, a few ideas on introducing The New Kitten to your current cat. Introducing The New Kitten to a resident cat may be slightly complex. Let your other cats walk around the carrier and look at The New

Kitten. For "holdouts," try not to rush things, but provide occasions where the older cats and The New Kitten can share pleasurable activities.

However, if you are not sure whether The New Kitten would have any disease that would infect your existing cat, you should first isolate the two of them for a while. If so, be sure to make The New Kitten feel at home, but also help your Siamese cat get used to the fact that he/she has a new sibling.

The New Kitten was having a hard time fitting in , but today our 3-year-old female cat decided to play mommy! Fred and The New Kitten are The New Kittens on the block! Salisbury and Quirkyartist are not. The New Sport being played by Twisted Princess 98 and the Star Wars Band is The New Kitten hunt.

About the Author, Realistic Internet Charley: "Don't worry. I am gonna kill The New Kitten. It won't quit crapping on the floor. I think we changed his name from Klaus to Killer. If it doesn't quit crapping on the floor, I'm changing my name to Killer. Anyway, right now I'm goin' to a Halloween party, so peace."

for Teresa Carmody

**The New Labels**

**The New Language**

50

**The New Language Poetry**

Evidently because the affiliation of The New Language
Poetry with the old renga seemed so appealing, it gave
11    poems The New Authority. Then, many groups of
poems and poetries (concrete poetry, women's poetry,
street poetry, etc.) came to be located outside of The
New Language Poetry.

**The New Left**

**The New Level**

**The New Liberty**

**The New Library**

**The New Light**

**The New Limerick**

**The New Line**


**The New Links**


**The New Literary Group**


**The New Look**

The New Look is about employment opportunities, new clothes, and sophisticated information, both The New Look and The New Look finder—as one can see reflected in The New Look. The New Look was one of the actresses of the time who wore The New Look with loose excess. The New Look is about how to be More Attractive! It's Time to Energize Your Soul, NOW! The New Look is a Simplicity Costume. Simplicity! It's So Easy!

The New Look is The New Look of Media. It's a web development and graphic design company. La plus importante enseigne de l'optique au Québec et au Canada. The most important banner of optics in Quebec and Canada. The New Look is about looking at The New Look. The New Look is seeing The New Look!

The stress of the job—so well hidden for much of the past six years—has begun to show on the old face of The New Look. But Look! Hello, I'm The New Look, and I recently joined the team as a Program Manager working on user experience. In anticipation of our next major pre-release and with the help of NASA's Spitzer Space Telescope, astronomers have conducted the most comprehensive structural analysis of our galaxy and found The New Look. The New Look includes photos of museum artifacts, a glossary of terms and information.

I agree that the old look sucks bad, but I don't think it will last long. I think it was a PR stunt. The classic New Look will always be the most popular. With more than 60 years of a certain… shall we say, style behind us, we will all be getting The New Look. You can see a few images of The New Look in the 2007 Preview. If you've got a craving to see even more, I've created The New Look Xeons and Opterons, dual- and quad-core Xeons, even F-Socket Opterons that have taken on The New Look.

The New Look has had a re-design and I am impressed. It now has a look n' feel very much like that which I believe is actually and truly The New Look. The description of The luxurious New Look with a sumptuous silhouette and billowing silhouetteskirts is already in the archives. The New Look has made a move to tailor its program to fit the needs of individuals and to challenge them at their separate skill levels. Links to The New Look can be found everywhere referencing The New Look.

The New Look at the Old Earth is a vital resource for today. Its thesis encourages you to think analytically and to bring understanding to The New Look at the Old Earth.

I've slowly been working on The New Theme and     102
I think I've made some good progress today. Take
a look and tell me what you think. Things might
look different, but we made sure the new interface is
The New Look for The New Vibes! The New Vibes!     104
are quietly releasing an updated look and feel this
evening. Read about the release as you find out more
about The New Look. We want to be easy to use
for everyone. You may notice that a few things have
moved around. For instance: The New Edition has     32
arrived, and it looks different.

**The New Love**

According to Žižek, hate is The New Love; and Jesus
said: "If anyone comes to me and does not hate his
father and his mother, his wife and children, his
brothers, they have not The New Love!" If you've
ever read about The New Love, you've probably
encountered a well organized, good read, and The
New Chapters on ethics and jealousy are great. The     17
New Love and Sex covers an enlarged view of The
New Work(s) being accomplished by The New Love.     108
The New Love holds the secret to sustainable intimate
relationships founded upon The New Love and Sex.

Introducing The New Love.

Polyamory: The New Love without limits. The Sacred
Space Institute is a place for The New Love, with
tantra, polyamory, The New Love without limits,
viacreme, workshops, love, sexual healing, orgasms,
sex and the spirit. In The New Love study, researchers

compared two sets of images, one taken when the participants were looking at a photo of a friend, and the other when The New Love was on a boat with movie stars, TV personalities, celebs, and more. Introducing, The New Love: At some point it will become necessary to introduce your man (forgive the gender). The New Love of my life. Isn't she glorious? She arrived around noon today. I carefully disrobed her and then felt a bit guilty.

Hate Is The New Love, The New Love and Sex excerpted from The New Love and Sex. The New Love triangle—the laptop slides into bed, in love... The New Love and Sex. Lust is The New Love when you're 29 years old, female, living in Long Island, New York, United States. Sticks & stones may break my bones but whips & chains Xite me. The New Love without Limits: Polyamory.

At some point it will become necessary to introduce your man (forgive the gender bias, but hey! I'm a girl!). People who like The New Me also like The New Love of my life. Say Hello to The New Love in my life. Her name is Patina. I got one of those dual core processors, so I'm curious how that'll work out. Also, I got a TV tuner. Meet The New Year's Resolution on The New Love: we'll find The whole New Generation of songs about love. Each song, hand selected for its heartfelt expression. Hate Is the New Love. An ideologue is a person who believes very strongly in particular principles and tries to follow them carefully.

**The New Love Poem**

The majority of critics and readers alike give themselves up to the enjoyment of The New Love Poem with a sigh of relief, accepting it as a gift from God, but Jack & Jill have mixed feelings about The New Love Poem. The New Love Poems selected from the anthology are, mostly, love letters from a husband to his wife. All rights reserved. Reprinting, reproducing, or translating The New Love Poem has shown to be a regular problem that influences The New Love Poem.

I should have put The New Love Poem first. I meant to. You will find The New Love and you will be joyful.     53
The New Love Poem is known for its honesty. The New Love Poem says I don't love you, but you can still be happy in your life.

Disclaimer: The New Love Poem and quote belong to their respective authors. If you want to use The New Love Poem and quote you should shop for The New Love Poem at our safe, secure, discreet, buy now, save money on every The New Love Poem purchase and get free shipping, we have The New Love Poem at this site, we have, have, have it, The New Love Poem.

The New Love Poem remembers the old love poem, but The New Love Poem is known for its honesty. The New Love Poem says I don't love you. The New Love

Poem remembers the old love poem in which a body is directly linked to the site of The New Love Poem.

One advantage at the centre of The New Love Poem is its ability to inspire a particular behavior in members of the listening and/or other audience members which is that after hearing or reading The New Love Poem, most people want to lick each other.

**The New Lyric**

**The New Machine**

**The New Manuscript**

42    **The New Me (see The New I)**

**The New Media State**

#2 Globally brand New Mexico as The New Media State. #3 Promote New Media business products and services to the local, regional, national, and international levels. #1 If an offer/answer/transaction succeeds, then The New Media State becomes active. I have never heard about a "proposed" media state.

If an offer/answer/transaction succeeds, The New Media State becomes active. I have never heard about a "proposed" media state… it isn't written anywhere. All those people back East may one day get on the wagon train and become a citizen of The New Media State. And if they don't, many of their children will.

Despite the explosion of The New Media State, television, due to its monopoly and to the absence of an adequate system of press distribution is by far the media state. The New Media State is selected by incrementing the media state by +1 and the disk access parameters associated with The New Media State are set up. The New Media State, where now each media is hype-linked to sites related to the media context as well as to the user context. The user can now provide The New Media State of spelling as effectively as the opposite of the birth of printing—undoing the crystallisation of spelling, and taking it back to The New Media State of fluid.

**The New Metaphor**

**The New Meter**

**The New Metonymy**

A few points, 1) The New Metonymy guidelines have superseded the older pilot projects… B) The New Metonymy guidelines indicate that well-defined geographical procedures are needed in order to re-install glass.

You are logged in to The New Metonymy and can use The New Metonymy to stave off any greatly appreciated guests.

## The New Model

## The New Motherfuckers

This is a musical concert featuring The New New Wave Sound of fifty on their heels from San Diego and The New Motherfuckers from Los Angeles. The New Motherfuckers are a spiritual band of cosmic proportions. For those of you who missed the show, The New Motherfuckers are everyone. Only God knows what The New Motherfuckers will do next.

The New Motherfuckers are in Los Angeles, California, the United States, the space where the beef is. The New Motherfuckers, The NMf, are our number one sound. I've only seen The New Motherfuckers once before and I already know them. If you're concerned about The New Motherfuckers and The New Collapse, read, and do some forward thinking about Love and Peace.

I've decided to load up some of you people with The New Motherfuckers, The brand New Echo from a few months ago. My profile of The New Motherfuckers shows what they are, a band from LA whom I saw at The Attack. You remember the old motherfuckers from the golden hill with fifty of The New Motherfuckers on their heels? Thank you to all those who turned out, The Attack was termed a success.

With fifty on their heels, The New Motherfuckers lounged with El Cid, clutching Roxy between them. The New Motherfuckers with fifty on their heels and Ken at the Club fending off the fifty on their heels with a zerox. The Smell was hot and you could hear the echo of The New Motherfuckers singing HOORAY!!! When the golden sun set, The New Motherfuckers were at a block party with the Youngs. Their Masters and Slaves were On the Rox. After the set, I was on my way to home base and walked over to Ken at the Club for a zerox. You will definitely see me tonight and all I can say is thank god I have The New Motherfuckers.

The New Motherfuckers have been zeroxed, The New Motherfuckers have been fortified—they show results, not post punk junk. The New Motherfuckers are in Hollywood. Hotlanta is in on The New Motherfuckers and Abe Vigoda tells how The New Motherfuckers come on and off superfast. Find more information on The New Motherfuckers from The New Motherfuckers, whom I've never heard of, but they're like a pointed cherry.

I assume The New Motherfuckers will play a live set after Fred and Octavius talk about giant haystacks. The New Motherfuckers have some very low-quality recordings available on the internet for your listening pleasure. They were recorded dictation-style by a couple giant haystacks. What's the hold-up on The New Fuckin' Song? Too lame to make music anymore guys?? God, The New Motherfuckers are online. My new The New Motherfuckers are online, HOORAY!!! Someone call Ron Johnson, 'cause both these bands must've heard an entire catalog of something. This session is alive and much much more... There's a menagerie of little labeled things: little radio, perfik, Peter and the Wolf, radio perfik, tim burgess, The New Motherfuckers… they come on and off superfast.

This amused me, it was from The New Motherfuckers, but I can't read: Listen everyone, the pixels have not formed in the house, but there is a frozen body along with The New Motherfuckers and certainly the big flame. The big bog is agape with The New Motherfuckers—Bark Bark Bark in the Smooth Groves and the Smell of a Bull smeared on the faces of The Royal Gents like Softboiled Eggies. The scene is full of prayers behind a bar in Glendale for The New Motherfuckers.

I can't read ya supercreep, you smell like a juiced sasquatch Mr. Sirhan Sirhan.

Supercreep is bringing The New Smell on Friday, slanderin' Los Creepers at the Spring Valley Moose Lodge with fifty on their heels like Jakked Rabbit Atoms. The New Motherfuckers has been cancelled.

for The New Motherfuckers

**The New Movements**

**The New Myth**

**The New Names**

**The New Narrative**

To talk about The New Narrative, I also have to talk about The New Narrative put in place by the time the elements of service were new. The central difficulty of writing The New Narrative is easy to The New Narrative, is notable, and sometimes The New Narrative emerges when facts previously unknown come to light.

The New Narrative that emerged last week was provided by those few chosen to add The New Narrative branches and help keep everything alive after a major shift to The New Narrative branch. A character may find form in The New Narrative forms. I recently received notice of The upcoming New Narrative.

I've never been to The New Narrative, but it looks like The very New Narrative approach to working with books by authors for the first time on the Internet. The New Narrative is: all available flight logs. The New Narrative: the alleged fleet of. It seems we've been here before.

Much as the narrative was emerging and nearing its 150th anniversary, The New Narrative found a need for the 21st Century. Process is in need—move the details. More on The New Narrative or persistence of vision, I am interested in a dialogue about The New Narrative, which is perhaps not so much new as newly theorized. Many prose writers do not consider themselves in The New Narrative age. The emerging narrative age is not a mere extension of the information age, but rather a distinct apparition driven by the Now, the time to offer The New Narrative using an alternative recipe.

The need for The New Narrative is a great opportunity for The progressive New Narrative approach to working, unraveling the mystery and the pervasive development of The New Narrative for Corporate Law discussing why we should care about biodiversity. Searching for The New Narrative, this article has taken a more pessimistic belief about the need to find The New Narrative, to justify its existence. Retelling and comprehension using The New Narrative develops the resource of The New Narrative. The more things change, the more things become The New Narrative. By introduction, fiction is a literature. The New Narrative Home is an anthology of original writings. To understand The New Narrative, an excerpt from *Changing Minds* has already changed your mind. *Old Tales in The New Narrative: Rethinking the Story of a Revolution*. Old Tales in The New Narrative all face not only difficult living conditions but also the disdain of civilians and the many.

**The New Natural**

**The New Naturalism**

**The New New**

**The New New Deal**

The New New Deal reform pits reactionaries against progressives. The New New Deal also implies some major long-run spending. First, Social Security would pay all its accrued benefits all at once. To keep the United States solvent through the 21st Century, we need to rethink Social Security, the tax structure, and health care.

Insurers have learned to pinpoint risks and avoid them. With computer models that can test a quake's effects on your house there's no need for scientists. There is no sturdier liberal or Democratic slogan than, "Jobs, Jobs, Jobs!" But liberals have a problem: The old capitalist job-production machine cannot simply be a well-planned reconstruction of The New Orleans. We need to set the stage for a comprehensive legislative initiative akin to The New Deal.

73

27

It's Time for The New New Deal.
...
Time for The New New Deal.

In three sections entitled "The Resilient," "Beyond Finance," and "The New New Deal," this speech draws heavily on a sense of history. The New New

Deal is about benefits alongside bankruptcy. The New New Deal will create The New Republic of American Liberalism, the permanent majority party with The New Vision that goes by various names: the unowned society, The New Deal, and The New New Deal.

Following an incredible amount of volunteer labor hours and energy, this dream was realized when we at last saw the opening of The New New Deal Café where people drink coffee and tea they haven't paid for and are asked to simply stare into space all day. After three or four hours of this difficult, back-breaking labor, they're given another cup of coffee or tea in a to-go cup—they are welcome to return after they've taken a good long nap.

The New New Deal is upon us. The President can either lead the charge or be run over by it. This upsurge will be called The New New Deal, and it presents a plan to deal with... The New New Deal! One of our greatest frustrations is when we collectively get wrapped up in theoretical discussions about the end of reform and The New New Deal and liberalism in recession and war. The New New Deal shows that President Bush's Social Security proposal is dead in the water—and that's a good thing too. The plan was half-baked and, fiscally speaking, without bankruptcy The New New Deal would just be The old New Deal in disguise. The New Republic of The New New Deal is original. It represents solid economic engineering and a straightforward time of progress in The New Era of The New New Deal.

Where's The New New Deal? Where are the sweeping reforms that the Democrats are all touting? They're nowhere. They can't even decide on a Presidential candidate. Finally, The New New Deal will speculate on the degree to which The re-crafted New Deal could serve as an organizing model for a liberal comeback of The New New Deal. The New New Deal talks about The Rabbit Going Back in The Hat, The Dance of the Crackpots, Welcoming the Enemy, and The Ride of the Wild Rabbit—summarizing a wide variety of ambitious but viable projects to improve all of our country by launching what's called The New New Deal. 27

The New Republic of The New New Deal will be mindful of both the successes and disappointments of The old New Deal of the 1930s. A multipronged plan founded upon bankruptcy—The New New Deal! Conservatives and small-government types are going to be run over by The New New Deal! 86

27

for Stan Apps

## The New New Wave Sound

The Angry Mob is based on the word uttered softly by yours truly—'No!'—and it reaches beyond The New New Wave Sound (think of bravery and etcetera). Also, I love butterflys, they rule. Indeed, while your band has allied itself with The New New Wave Sound, it has more in common with the era of Isolation Drills guided by the Authoritative Voice of Franz Ferdinand. These guys are definitely talented, they sound like what I would call Canada's offering to The New New Wave Sound coming out of Britain. But with the badd business of their second-rate songs, the boys have ditched The New New Wave Sound in favor of a spiteful ska riff reminiscent of the era of tragic kingdoms.

Are you into God? because she rules, and if you like The New New Wave Sound, check out The Rapture. With the coming of The New Dawn, the trembling of a white rose in the wind gleefully wreaks havoc on the idea of the concept album—as well as the retro-futurism of The New New Wave Sound. One of the first things to make it into The New New Wave Sound, employment has often been compared to the cure, but it's turned out to be more like the breakdown.

**The New New York School**

The New New York School has issued a Limited-Time Offer! Yes! Sign me up for Vanity! Issue me 12 tickets to the Fair for only $15 … a savings of 72%. The New New York School will bring The New Times of Vanity to the York Fair, where all the Art and Artists of the year will be. The New New York School, a talent show, an affair of Vanity and Musak.

In the December 2006 issue of Vanity Fair magazine, artist Kehinde Wiley is featured as one of eight young art talents in The New New York School who have, in talking about that other contact sport, Flarf, mentioned the Language school of writing and The New New York School. How, exactly, can The New New York School deal with the following comments made by the chancellor, "What? Any new school that we open there's added police security. Uh-huh!"

...ashbery poeticity differend pantoum schuyler orphic nonrational taxonomia cataphoric altieri lautreamont diaristic... This is either the Last Poem of the New York School or the First Poem of The New New York School, probably both.

The New New York School of December 2006 is in video footage from the Andy Warhol Factory reunion photo shoot. Library Media Examination Specialist and Fine Arts Professor Paul Fabozzi has used museomania and developed scoring norms for The New New York School.

Kristin Baker (BFA '98), named one of eight young artists to watch in The New New York School, compared this Vanity Fair to the classical work of Aeschylus, as it was being resuscitated by The New New York School. Padgett has said of appropriation: It was fun, yeah. We could all be The New New York School! I call deKooning, I want to be deKooning! You can be Pollock. These buildings harbor the ghosts of a thousand kinds of things.

**The New Night**
Hello Evereybody! I am happy to launch The New Night!

The New Night is a passage from one life to another.

To begin with, The New Night bears little relation to the television series I watched with my grandmother. Father's mother and I saw The New Night full of

other skies of other sizes: small, medium, large—
completely original.

What The New Night does have is the potential to
be The New Night on the town. The New Night
rides like a movie in an egg, like a fast car. To take
full advantage of it, you should use nightclubs, food,
drink, hotels and everything in between. Take a look
at The New Night, the Sky! ... The Night has been
growing and expanding.

Welcome to The New Night, the domain for the
passage of The Night.

The New Night is like a leopard, a more compact,
high quality night with super fast, high resolution
vision. The New Night has the power of a canon, the
equivalent of a flash shot into the Sky. Fully original,
it comes in all sizes: small, medium, and large. The
New Night will revolutionize bodybuilding by filling
that crucial time and sweeping the nation.

I think if robbers are smart (and I hope they aren't),
then they would be crazy enough to make the middle
of the day The New Night. The all-nighter is The New
Rite of Passage for young professionals. Who ever
thought working so hard could be so much punch,
so much life? In Manchester they don't live in the sky,
they live in The New Night.

The New Night is a time sequencing service. Herald
morning sequencing! You are here: The New Night.

The New Night is crib swimming. At about 1 a.m.
this morning, Zion started a full out crawl-stroke in

the crib. My sister is in town for the weekend, and she offered to watch Adam if Beth and I wanted to go out for a while. In this respect, The New Night will bring legislation focusing on empowering women who are not interested in standard daytime jobs.

Ok cast, crew and viewers, here is The New Night. Right off the bat, the filmmakers knew they wanted to cast Ben Stiller in the lead role of the hapless, yet ultimately heroic, guard of The New Night. The New Night is not up to the standards of either series, but what show on television today is? If picked up, The New Night would be part of the lineup and would be produced by Television. Alternatively, if performance is expected to improve with The New Night and The New Vision Capability, the comparison of night-versus-day from the previous stage must take place on a daily basis.

104

Network! Network! The New Night has gone from TV to comics and back again.

Are weekends becoming too expensive? Ever wonder how to make your date without breaking the bank? The New Night is a program at the Museum of New York's American Museum of Natural History which has been so popular that all available dates have sold out. Attila the Hun and his pals exhibit creatures up top, like the 20th Century Fox, and make things a bit tense for The New Night. I don't think the show was all that bad, but I really wish I had more time to find The New Night.

The New Night follows a circular path that goes toward the Sacramento River on West Sacramento

Avenue, down Nord Avenue and then The New Night goes downtown. The New Night is the official time of Rembrandt—Rembrandt Harmenszoon Van Rijn is generally accepted as the most important Dutch to watch The New Night from year to year, focusing on the release of light walking through The New Night.

**The New Nonsense**

**The New Norm**

**The New Nostalgia**

**The New Nothing**

**The New Numerical Evaluations**

**The New Object**

**The New Objectivism**

## The New Old

As the pool of young recruits dries up, companies and countries are putting the retired back to work, focusing on all the technical, nitty-gritty jobs. They make up 30% of North America's population and are its most powerful demographic. They're in their 40s, 50s, and 60s, but they only show up as The New Old in journalism—print stories, e-mail stories, rants and raves.

The New Old is an agenda-setting report presenting the initial findings of a joint project between Dems and those highly concerned with age. The report explores how the closer and more intently we look at nature, the more species we find, at home and in places like the heart of Borneo. Despite the deluge of minimalist magazine images as slick as a well-licked plate, there are countless reasons to preview all the articles and books about The New Old. Listen to this article published originally in 3-Column Format, translated into The New Old.

Ideas, as they come sync'd up, wired in and ready to head out into the world, can be identified by eight principles that make The New Old something just outside of tradition, yet still timeless. The New Old leopard... The New Old leopard.

The New Old is very funny... all about media, news-papers, The New York Review of Capitalist Undergarments, The New Special, The Old-Fashioned Way and The New Old—measuring fluid ounces by fluid ounces. 98

I was all choked up saying goodbye, when I should have just closed with "until next time, The New Old."

Boys' clubs and social networking sites are flooding cyberspace and attracting huge investments, let's take a look and see whether they're worth The New Old or even electronic money, and whether or not they're accepting all major credit cards with secure transactions. With less private money in the market and with the dot-com halo gone, investors will be more patient and innovation will go back to what it always has been, The New Old. The New Old isn't the Amazon economy, it isn't networks. It's institutions, and the organizational transformation of American manufacturing. It's books, nostalgia, memory, and the history of the Lower East Side.

Money returns like an image of not so long ago.

108    The New Old is The New West, a family paradise complete with horseback riding, singing cowboys, and roaring fires… an inconvenient response and its Battletech objectification of the frontier lands—a text-based, real-time version of the popular Battletech game where players take to the front lines in a brutal World of The New Old. The old ceremony was our one mistake

The New Old is a world living beyond myth.

The New Old is The American Spectator. The New Old, Aha! Weird American Mind Control, I Presume… Bon Appetit. Hello, from The New Old!

for Harold Abramowitz

**The New Old English**

**The New Orleans**

**The New Package**

**The New Pantoum**

Jolly Teabags! The New Pantoum doesn't need its oil changed! Imagine that! The New Pantoum is an amazing lubricant.

The New Pantoum is The topical New Challenge, the previous topic was La Pixie Strangiato. The Challenge challenged duration. The New Topic will be Alone. 17

103

I copied The New Pantoum and placed it in The New Pantoum. I've just created this—enjoyed it.

And The New Pantoum doesn't need its oil changed! Imagine that!

**The New Paper**

**The New Parable**

**The New Paragraph**

**The New Past**

**The New Pattern**

**The New Pattern Poem**

There is a brief summary for the production and rhythm of The New Pattern Poem, and a statement that The New Pattern Ci and Qu are among the metrical verse.

**The New Pen**

**The New People**

**The New Person**

**The New Phrenology**

Address the question of localization: whether psychological processes can be defined and isolated in a way that permits them to be associated with *The New Phrenology. The Limits of Localizing Cognitive Processes in the Brain (Life and Mind: Philosophical Issues in Biology and Psychology): The New Phrenology.* Having just done a posting on MRI-MRI, I thought it appropriate to point to a discussion by Michael Shermer about *The New Phrenology and The Limits of Localizing Cognitive Processes in the Brain.* In *The New Phrenology,* William R. Uttal (2001) explores the fundamental question, "Is Cognitive Neuroscience The New Phrenology?" (Introduction by Professor Bill Uttal and Professor Michael Posner). Professor Bill Uttal responds with a précis of *The New Phrenology and The Limits of Localizing Cognitive Processes in the Brain.* Source: Author Uttal, W. R., Brain and Mind, Volume 3, Number 2. STARR. Discussed in the current *Popular Science Monthly*: the question of the old and The New Phrenology. There is one consideration which seems easily disproved. This book is an exhaustive review of arguments for the negative answer to one of the most fundamental questions of psychology: Can psychological processes be physically located? *The New Phrenology: the Limits of Localizing Cognitive Processes in the Brain.* Edited by W. R. Uttal (Pp 255, £27.50), published by MIT Press, USA, 2001, William R. Uttal's *The New Phrenology* is a broad attack on localization in cognitive neuroscience. He argues that even though the brain is a highly differentiated network, to gain access to it please either Log In, Activate your complimentary web account, or if you are a print subscriber, subscribe now. American intellectuals argue that New, noninvasive imaging technologies allow us to observe the brain while it is actively engaged in mental activities. Uttal cautions, however, that in the Amazon he came to experiment with distributed neural systems, beyond *The New Phrenology*. ISBN: 9781597380195: William R. Uttal: Books & Book Symposiums: William R. Uttal's *The New Phrenology. A Précis of The New Phrenology: The Limits of Localizing Cognitive Processes in the Brain*. ... Apr 12, 2007 ... The New Phrenology: The question is, could it have some of the same ideologies about race, class, gender, and even religion and other forms, in a nutshell? Uttal is arguing that the modern imaging technologies (eg, fMRI) are toys used by cognitive neuroscientists that are following their theories in a free article about *The New Phrenology: The Limits of Localizing Cognitive Processes in the Brain*. Access the article at My Library.com: *The New Phrenology: the Limits of Localising Processes in the Brain* by W. R. Uttal. (Pp. 255; £27.50.) MIT Press: London. 2001. *Psychological Medicine & The New Phrenology*. The New Phrenology summary with encyclopedia entries, research information, and more. The New Phrenology (face=Bold+) Bookmarks (Face=Bold-) The New Phrenology (face=Bold+) Encyclopedia. com (face=Bold-). *The New Phrenology: The Limits of Localizing Cognitive Processes in the Brain (Life & Mind: Philosophical Issues in Biology & Psychology)* from the Amazon care of the UK. W. R. Uttal: *The New Phrenology*, find Psychotherapy Networker articles. (face=Bold+) Bookmarks (face=Bold-) (face=Bold+) The New Phrenology (face=Bold) (face=Italic+) *The New Phrenology: The Limits of Localizing Cognitive Processes in the Brain (Life and Mind: Philosophical Issues in Biology and Psychology)* (Paperback) Brain Imaging: is it The New Phrenology? National

Undergraduate Research Clearinghouse #2 Available online at http://www.webclearinghouse.net/volume/ *The New Phrenology: the Limits of Localizing Cognitive Processes in the Brain* reviewed by G. Rees, full text. The full text of this article is available at Barnes & Noble. Find *The New Phrenology* by William R. Uttal. Enjoy book clubs, author videos and customer reviews. Free 3-Day shipping on $25 orders! *The New Phrenology: The Limits of Localizing Cognitive Processes. The New Phrenology* will be especially useful for consumers (as opposed to producers). All about *The New Phrenology: The Limits of Localizing Cognitive Processes in the Brain (Life and Mind: Philosophical Issues in Bi)* by William R. Uttal. Objective Testing, *The New Phrenology* by F. C. Osenburg. Blind confidence in the capacity of the scientific method to solve all problems of the scientific method is problematic. Science or The New Phrenology? If the Lord Almighty had consulted me before embarking on Creation, I should have recommended something simpler.

for Dan Richert

## The New Physicality

Culture is a Physical Movement, along with Religion, Race, Gender, Politics, and The New Physicality; the Dénouement will come in the form of Ideology and the Cult of the Body.

The hardest thing to deal with when I was writing my book on the Resurrection was to talk about the new kind of love video made by soft skull (avatars are The New Physicality) and probably some other delinquents (always with the lies), as well as the installations brought on by a laymen's profession of love (quite possibly The New Physicality or corporeality will bring with it a heightened concern for the body and the senses, relieved of the practical restrictions of urban life).

The New Physicality will come in the form of Dance, The New Physicality that no choreographer has explored, as dance, just as Isadora Duncan's earth-bound movement foretold The New Physicality of Martha Graham. In this postmodern form I experience The New Physicality, in interactions with other dancers arising directly out of object work, it all coincides with the day, and it carries a powerful if embryonic rawness that springs from the shock of immediate conflict between the old spirituality and The New Physicality.

So, in our time, composers have emerged who reverse this process through dancing and listening, and The New Physicality of expression has shown up between the dynamic solo styles of both. They are practicing the art of internal energy manipulation, the essence of creation in The New Physicality.

Antonin said about The New Physicality of long distance love: there is no chance we will fall apart, there is no chance, there are no parts.

The immateriality/materiality division has been reshuffled.

Even in the passage just quoted, Artaud affirms The New Physicality of language that can be achieved only in the *mise en scène,* the operational site for recordkeeping in The New Physicality. Again, it is useful to cite Brandt, who explains that not all aspects of The New Physicality and the emphasis on passions were valorized.

What 60 page thesis is on paper? These milennial reports are, and are many and are on paper too—on the resurrected One's encounter with the disciples as fact. However, we can in no way imagine The New Physicality of the resurrected One wrung from the painful tension between the old spirituality and The New Physicality.

Much like a small rudder steers a large comment, the two previous ones, taken together (one about The New Physicality and the other about The New Cultural Productivity), should be explicated in terms of finding words to describe The New Physicality. 27

But to whom?

To these modern women. *La Barre du jour,* in the summer of 1977, conveyed both The New Physicality of women's writing and the extent to which the expression of this physicality hit upon The New Physicality. So many spectators surrendered to the rediscovery of the human and The New Physicality In Late Medieval Art & Literature.

I pray that none of the aces show, again and again, while the writings on the American cinema of the interwar period stress The New Physicality, the exterior surface or outer skin of things, a comprehensive transition has reconstituted The New Physicality as the desire for self-determination fundamental to the American ethos as the nation steps uncertainly into the next decade.

Label inspiration, thinking, ubicomp, and the logically viewed user interface as operational sites for The New Physicality of recordkeeping.

The immaterial-material division has been reshuffled.

As Maribeth Lohan went on to track the action of innate intelligence in the creation, transmission and expression of Power, The New Physicality provided a nice, energetic interface.

## The New Piss

## The New Plague

## The New Plan

## The New Platonic Love

It would be surprising if he had taken much stock in The New Platonic Love of the précieuses. That he shows the influence of the cult is no doubt true.

**The New Pleasure**

**The New Poetic Voice**

We'd better hurry, The New Poetic Voice is following closely on that of another past master of the genre. The return to quality grows out of The New Poetic Voice: the condition of the poet's solitude and the authenticity of the poet's private vision. It will come to grow out of the ashes of which The New Poetic Voice will arise.

Among some of the characteristics of The New Poetic Voice is an increased reliance on the language of the people and a commitment to choose poetic themes that show a profound shift in lyric person and attitude. The New Poetic Voice of the 1960s was not that of self-searching individuals. The New Poetic Voice led, by its great power, to The Mask of Anarchy, a remarkably accessible voice, indeed rather common, crude even.

In the first of these texts, the seemingly unthinkable happens: Prince Deathless quotes an oft-quoted passage from "Song of Myself" indicating The New Poetic Voice that Walt Whitman attempted to construct in his *Leaves of Grass*: "Do I contradict the discernible features of The New Poetic Voice?"

**The New Politics**

**The New Powers**


**The New Present**


**The New Problem**


**The New Process**


**The New Project**


**The New Prose**


**The New Prose Poem**

The New Prose Poem invaded The American Prose Poem with Poetic Form and the Law of Genre. In the hands of The Language Poets, The New Prose Poem insisted on its scriptural illegibility rather than a speech-based comprehensibility. When rewriting the sentence with the language and poetry of The New Prose Poem, does language control like money? If you ask two student volunteers to read The New Prose Poem, and then ask students to discuss a few leading questions: How does the sound of the poem change?

Kathy Acker has created an Empire of the Senseless.

The New Prose Poem has emerged as the methodological culmination of the transgeneric experiments dealt with in the figurative chapters of *The Best of the Prose Poem*. In an unreal essay that is itself a Miniature Art, Charles Simic rewrites the sentence in the language of poetry and The New Prose Poem. In The New Prose Poem, suffuse with the business of falling asleep, he writes: "To brave the day turning outward like an ear, too polite to hear."

One of the most apparent sites in which one can observe this tense complementarity of modernist and documentary modes is in The New Prose Poem genre that Ron Silliman's *Ketjak* marks as The New Stage in the group tendency, from a non-referential 98 minimalism to The New Prose Poem. He has been busy lately, preparing The New Prose Poem and The New Sentence: a Journal of Prose Poetics, to be 89 released this weekend with Big Poetry.

An international journal, or even an issue of *Sentence: A Journal of Prose Poetics* (one of The New Prose Poem journals), takes us then to The New Prose Poem, a movement advocated by Kitagawa around 1927/29, and realised by the poets belonging to The New Literary Group. In 1928 he was associated with the 51 magazine *Poetry and Poetics*. He was also associated with The New Prose Poem. Who, for instance, remembers that Victor de Laprade was France's foremost poet in the mid-nineteenth century, at the very time when The New Prose Poem formed out of language and poetry?

The second part of this volume alphabetically lists postmodern authors and critics, giving biographical summaries and a brief rewriting of The New Sentence and The New Language Poetry.

89
50

Streets that lead nowhere in particular and which characters walk along aimlessly herald the appearance in nineteenth-century France of The New Prose Poem. And with the attention initiated now, I am happy to read this poem, which, by the way, is not in any book, but is forthcoming in the fall in *The New Prose Poem*, a diaristic journal of The New Sentence.

89

## The New Psychoanalysis

## The New Quatrain

This is also the *ihh* sound which occurs in each line of The New Quatrain and gives it a lighter, singing tone lending a continuity to the preceding quatrains. The New Quatrain illustrates the poet's neutrality vis-a-vis the subject. Those who keep their reason but lie to the clouds by denying them—stanza fifteen is also revised—pave the way for The New Quatrain. The poet sought the ear of Christ on these mad things. And then, in the white pavilion, when the poet, with the old remark about gleaning abandoned, placed The New Quatrain about the greedy master in place—what had happened in the meantime? It was The New Quatrain consisting of four phrases in a column shape. The New Quatrain and logo have

been used this year in The New Inauguration. And    46
now, take the Now out of line 17, starting The New
Quatrain with "The day." Other than those two
minor things, it was a very well written poem. Some
of The New Quatrain pieces are opulent and highly
detailed. The New Company, which specializes in     23
accurate reproductions of grand antiques, has bought
The New Quatrain. Usagi spoke as she was thinking
about The New Quatrain of the prophecy. "I don't
know Usagi-san." Hotaru spoke, "Indeed they would
like to remove The New Quatrain. Ours, as well as
The New Quatrain just given, also deals with the
Pope changing countries (and possibly the Church),
Roman guards in torment/panic, clouds nuclear...

**The New Rabbit**

**The New Readers**

**The New Real**

**The New Realism**

**The New Reason**

**The New Record**

**The New Rejection Letter**

Regarding the appended observations, which are called The Principal Reasons for the rejection, are e-mails The New Rejection Letter or should these also be regarded as a sign that these folks actually have me in the "watch for the future" pile? You got The New Rejection Letter, which translated means: Your domain sucks, why did you submit it to GreatDomains? Please do not do it again. It also said something about "so what does everyone think about The New Rejection Letter?" I remember getting excited at first because I thought... Now I'm not saying this right, but with this being the email age, not responding to your email is The New Rejection Letter. I have responded to many ads from the appeals committee, but their concerns about the wording in The New Rejection Letter are out of hand—their discussion focused only on the second paragraph. In The New Rejection Letter one finds a similar statement.

**The New Repetition**

**The New Republic**

**The New Rhyme**

**The New Rhythm**

**The New Rite of Passage**

**The New Romance**

**The New Romanticism**

**The New Rondeau**

With open doors or without open doors, all is shown in The New Rondeau. Below is the 2002 LeMans Bentley Gold Line model: built out and in kit form.

View The New Rondeau report at the rondeau report. The red team built up one episode of The New Rondeau. They wrote that "Madamme Lange sang The New Rondeau we composed," which is a reference to performance #K.416 on July 2nd of the same year.

The September report of The Department of State Office on the Wastewater from Wildwood Estates claimed that an inverted siphon would be required across the open marsh, the main force of which would spread through the area and morph it into The New Rondeau.

## The New Rose

## The New Sapphic

The New Sapphic: Some Like It Hot.

Among The New Sapphic fragments of special interest is the beautiful "ostrakon ode," a simple poem on feminine attire.

The Independent Cinema has brought The New Ethnicities into the hall of critical dialogues. The world of Independent Film and Video has made The New Sapphic into a series! Some Like It Hot: The Cinema of The New Sapphic.

Click here to get a Full Version of The New Sapphic. Download The New Sapphic. In addition, also get the latest applications, TV shows, movies, and games.

So the days multiply, caught here in the devil's windpipe, where winds hoot. (See The New Sapphic tag, unwrap out of mummy's rags.) I have information on The New Sapphic sex, The New Sapphic sex is best! I have seen all the Internet... Anything.

**The New Saturn**

**The New Science of Society**

**The New Seasons**

**The New Sensation**

**The New Sense**

**The New Sensuality**

**The New Sentence**

An important talk on Grammar has become prosody, analyzing YOU in reference to The New Sentence. One out of two people here are taking part in a crime spree in which people submit The New Sentence. The New Sentence will be added to the corpus and given a preliminary rating. That rating will go up or down if The New Sentence is ordered. For who rented, created, or updated a man getting The New Sentence? Bring conviction to the chase! A panel ruled Friday that a judge must find The New Sentence for a convicted Sentence whose death was overturned last year by The New United Information of arbitrary sentencing. A federal judge Monday rejected detention of The New Sentence, ending five months of house arrest, and calling the sentence reasonable. For a killer to get The New Sentence it would take 90 deaths on the trail. Two life terms as the cost will lead people to stop fighting death. The original 24-year sentence appears and is appealing, and has rules based in part on miscalculated losses. For example: I know all the ways you hide and all the times you lied. The plans within the plans. The wheels. A man convicted in the acid attack could get The New Sentence. A convicted invader will get The New Sentence. A man has been sentenced. People are expected to return Friday to ask for The New Sentence. Meanwhile, Vermont state House Republicans introduced non-binding examples of sentences that can hide The New Sentence inside them when repeated quickly. Now, The New Sentence is beginning. The New Sentence is provided. Your The New Sentence should be The New Sentence. Anyone might be able to plant their spring garden after all the need for The New Sentence. This Act will establish the Risk as Authority creates The New Sentence for the High Order. The Lifelong Order of The New Sentence in exercise. You will change one sentence into another. For example, you will change: This car is his. into: This car is his. If you need help, The New Sentence will lower the sentence into the first word of The New Sentence. Superior orders are The New Sentence of a professional inquirer. Question leniency and get The New Sentence. For instance, begin The New Sentence. Put in a request for The

New Sentence. A federal judge ruled today that you must keep wearing The New Sentence. Business & Finance will win The New Sentence. Quoting is provided free by the culture, The New Sentence, and the politics of parataxis in the avant-garde from 1914 to 2001. Taken from the Critical Survey in Reference & Education Part II: The New Sentence modulates. Practice makes perfect.

**The New Sentimentality**

**The New Septenary**

Founded on the intellect and the crystalline truth about The New Septenary, the earth and the whole mass of these statements are free to buff the intermezzo of the four angels and the other angel; and then The New Septenary will introduce a group of trumpets to loosen the seventh seal.

**The New Serenade**

**The New Series**

### The New Sestina

Highlight: Jai with The New Sestina—shit! Werd. The feature. Damn, y'all. Martín is a pro. Punto. He went up there and rocked out.

### The New Sex

### The New Shit

### The New Simile

### The New Sky

Here's The New Sky, but it looks too fake.

It's 6 a.m. and I'm wide awake. This is, I've heard, the best time to ferret out low international fares on the Internet. You can follow the progress of Coventry City's new stadium as it's built on the site of an old gasworks in Holbrooks with a virtual tour of The New Sky.

The New Sky has provided the Sky with the opportunity to redesign its distinctive appearance and develop its weather.

At the opening of The New Sky in the city's Cultural Center and Haak´u Museum, two unique showcases will premier. One of the exhibits that promises to be attractive is The New Sky, it's also highly likely that the Sky will add a similar on-demand service that will be strongly coupled to The New Sky broad-vision-band-pro, again adding The New Sky refractors that contain one element made from Watchers.

Reach out and search for scientists.

Now, let's drag The New Sky into the original picture. Close the Sky so it is out of the way and click on the background layer of The New Sky, you'll see the indexing concept for huge astronomical catalogues and its realization for main astronomical queries, cone searches, The New Sky, and some new venture portals. What is behind the home portal of The New Sky? Here's The New Sky, but it looks too fake.

The New Sky needs tweaking.

Say the edge where The New Sky meets the old picture is hard and does not look right, when you paint it black you reveal more of The New Sky and blend the edges. The New Sky is the Dark Energy, the Dark Matter of this transient universe. Home is The New Sky.

Preview The New Sky now! The Awesome sound! The Stratosphere!

Images of telescopes have been updated by The New Sky. You can watch all four and their signature new art: White Like The New Sky, This View Is Breathtaking. The Outer Solar System is full of near-earth objects like The New Sky with large synaptic galleries.

31  No more Mister Nice Sky. John has no interest in The
    New Sky or The New Earth for their own sake, they
    merely set the stage for the real center of his attention,
46  The New Jerusalem, where we'll see The New Sky—
    four completed galleries of incredible space images
    available for viewing along with some soothing music.

A garden of lights links the old sky above to The New
Sky below.  Between the garden of lights above and
The New Sky below are two rooms and an expanse of
The New Sky.

Fact, The New Sky Produces Programmes, Forever—
that's four times more than the standard Sky.

Fact, The New Sky Has Full Sky Functionality plus.

Fact, The New Sky faces the Huangpu River, like The
New Sky of Pudong, on the other side of the old sky,
which didn't even exist fifteen years ago.

Customers like [this one] have found The New Sky.

The New Sky is a double-take inducing line of
sports cars, just as downtown, The New Sky is an
89  introduction to The New Saturn. And, as with the
    Solstice, the draw of The New Sky is its stunning body
    and low price tag—base priced at $24,000. Its design
    compares with plenty of sharp sports cars. These
    two-seat sports cars now have more astronomers at
    Arecibo Observatory hoping that The New Sky will
    result in a comprehensive census of galaxies out to a
    distance of 800 million light years.

## The New Slogan

## The New Smell

Once again The New Smell will wear off like it did a few years ago with once-hot nationwide phenoms like Jammin' Oldies and all '80s radio. I could hear the sleeping man snore.

It's The New Smell filed under cellphones and technology… ah, the aroma of technology phones. You have a phone where you need anything.

The New Smell routed all those other smells. The rich olfactory texture of the street was shattered. The New Smell pushes out the old and makes room for the new, like a fresh gust of wind. The New Smell is truly gorgeous!

In the past you might have had incidents like this and you couldn't even distinguish The New Smell from among all the pollutants. The smell seemed to have no center. I couldn't put my finger on what The New Smell was. It wasn't fishy, or salty or sweet, that is known: it was sort of bodily. I like The New Smell.

Let cats sniff at each other under a door. After awhile, let the cats meet. For the old dog to understand The New Smell, he should be let out of the cage as many times a day as possible. Use an automatic litter box, so once they get used to The New Smell, they're good to go. The old dog should only be let out after it is on a distinguished road. When you first bring

47 in The New Kitten, leave it in the cat carrier and let the other cats get used to The New Smell. Swap their cages (including litter boxes) every day or two; this acclimates them to The New Smell and teaches them

85 that The New Rabbit is not threatening. Or, rub The

47 New Kitten with a towel and then place the towel in the cat's bed to let the cat become accustomed to

47 The New Smell. The New Kitten has to get used to

105 The New Wallpaper, chair, sofa and television, and all the time give the pet plenty of attention and time to adjust to The New Smell and change. Bucks are also

31 interested in The New Doe and sometimes will begin grunting as they track down The New Smell. They urinate or defecate outside and do territorial marking. They may start marking in the baby's room. The New

11 Smell of The New Baby is very different. Have someone show the item to your pets and let them get used to The New Smell before it actually comes into your house.

I have used various Stayfree pads for many years and loved them, but The New Smell (which Stayfree is marketing as Odor Neutralizers) is an odor all the cats are used to.

20 I always find the scene of The New Clothes, so carefully laid out by a child for the first day of school, touching to the point of bringing tears to my eyes.

20 Giving (and receiving!) The New Clothes is a favorite holiday activity, but The New Smell that comes along

20 with The New Clothes often signals a presence. I love The New Smell that my children's back-to-school clothes have, but I've heard it's actually a sign of chemicals on the fabric. Is that true?

We think when we move into a new home, The New Smell in the air that we cannot see with our naked eye is actually the smell of radon gas. #2 When you come home, The New Items have some of The New Smell 46 and can add in good smells from time to time while making you feel better along the way. #1 Throw in a large ad for Media/TV, and keep the gaminess. #3 Repeat the process a second time, ringing a bell and walking around.

How long on average does The New Smell last in the car and is there a way to prolong its most welcome stay in your car? Go test drive The New Cars with 17 no intention of buying just for the experience of The New Smell. For one, The New Smell requirements might result in a huge rush to supply cabs with air fresheners that sometimes smell significantly worse than whatever.

There are certain people who are addicted to The New Smell. Recommended: No amount paid.

**The New Social Relations**

**The New Solitude**

**The New Song**

**The New Special**

**The New Sport**

**The New Sprung Rhythm**

Consonant with the solemnity of the theme and capable also of modulation without abruptness into a different measure, that is The New Sprung Rhythm.

**The New Stage**

**The New Stanza**

**The New Stasis**

**The New Status Quo**

**The New Story**

## The New Subjectivity

Craft has traditionally been interpreted as a combination of individual creativity and a closeness to materials or making. The New Craft, or My World of The New Subjectivity, turns to craft as a way of seeing beyond the global product framework that valorized The New Subjectivity of the warrior (which served to recast women as being of the home-front). The emergence of The New Subjectivity in contemporary design, as designers use sophisticated new technologies to do their work, is strongly informed by their distinct but complementary backgrounds. The New Subjectivity senses that private feelings are always related to collective feelings. 26

The term "Rosie the Rivetor" changed in social and literary sensibilities in the mid-seventies as manifested in the Greens, The New Subjectivity and reactions to consumer society. The New Subjectivity briefly recalls the nine-year process from the beginning that resulted in the love tapes and films which were only precursors to The New Subjectivity on display in documentary film and video of the 1980s and 1990s. In literature, the nimbus surrounding these decades was termed The New Subjectivity. Historically, the familiar evaluations haven't included The New Subjectivity and the same fate has befallen them as befell the Soviet regime in the 1980s which failed to respond to The New Subjectivity.

English industrial structuralism and The New Subjectivity, today create a space where it is common to be told that whatever is said is no more than The New Subjectivity. The failure of The New Subjectivity lies not merely in its vehicle. Certainly, lyrics like, "Once I cave in, what can I fight? I can never win My World" show The New Subjectivity in its design phase. In addition to being quite mystical, The New Subjectivity becomes a God-like presence that creates The New World. The logic here can be quite contradictory, particularly around debates on the emergence of The New Subjectivity.

The New Subjectivity created through ascetical practice may come about, but The New Subjectivity will more likely result from The New Social Relations and The New Symbolic artistic direction in the Contemporary Arts. Society must be capable of forming collective agencies of enunciation that match The New Subjectivity in such a way that it desires its own mutation. This will give us a glimpse into The New Subjectivity of humanity, which replaces the liberal humanist subjectivity of Enlightenment-based modernity.

The technology of the self, proposed as The New Subjectivity, is not a marginal phenomenon one finds only in evidence among members of the art world. Functioning as a linguistic marker coined originally by journalists, The New Subjectivity wasn't simply more rewarding than earlier forms of subjectivity, what was important was the moral prism. The New Subjectivity looks not only at the negative performances (rejecting wealth or sexuality), but primarily toward the positive articulation of The New Subjectivity that would be refracted accordingly. The New Subjectivity doesn't want to be aimed at the lucky minority of the well-informed.

Among the many formulations used to assume a subject, The New Subjectivity is the entrance and the awareness that makes The New Subjectivity that which we are trying to describe and invent at the same time. Attention thus becomes a fluctuating, floating dimension attached to The New Subjectivity that it also helps define.

Here's something new: you're reading an essay on The New Subjectivity.

The New Subjectivity, I conclude, is characterized by hybridity, delirium, automatism, and a troubling ambiguity between the self and its technological process. I also have a new house in Connecticut and I'm going to buy a car and be multiple, and finally be replaced by The New Subjectivity of postmodernism spawned on the Internet, the main representative of cyberspace.

**The New Superego**

**The New Surrealism**

**The New Symbolic**

**The New Symbolism**

**The New System**

**The New Talk**

**The New Tendency**

**The New Text**

**The New Theme**

**The New Theory**

**The New Theory of Colour**

**The New Times**

**The New Topic**

**The New Trope**

**The New Tsuba**

**The New United Information**

The New United Information, a future security component of the Department of Homeland Security, could become an ideal go-between for security researchers and vendors, but a panel of judges ruled on Friday that a Convinced Sentence must be found instead of The New Sentence whose 89 death was easily overturned last year by The New United Information.

**The New Unrequited Love**

I think for me The New Unrequited Love represents a man who I feel I can be me with, and who wants me for who I am, not "what I can do." The New Unrequited Love! Maniacs in Manhattan! More than usual, I mean! For those of you in NYC, the much-anticipated, the long-awaited… The New Unrequited Love.

104

**The New Verse**

**The New Version**

**The New Vibes**

**The New Villanelle**

(Not that some of them aren't still bad, The New Villanelle in particular, but hey, that's life!) And to top the news off, until I find out about my IP, I'm just gonna have to talk about me. For a while I knew someone / Who made me feel complete / Smiling now though she is gone / For a while she was the one / Who simply swept me off my feet.

**The New Virginity**

**The New Vision**

**The New Vision Capability**

I cannot recall one time when he used his headlights; perhaps they were too old for the current generation, so now everything is giving way to The New Vision Capability.

## The New Vocabulary

## The New Walk(ing)

## The New Wallpaper

## The New War

This week marks the anniversaries of three landmark events that paved the way for recent developments. With all the fuss about Barack Obama and Hillary Clinton, John Edwards' presidential campaign might look like a long shot. So, at this time there is a little relief and we have a pleasant topic instead of The New War.

The National Press Club in Washington, D.C. presented a discussion forum on Religion and Public Life delivering nonpartisan, timely information on issues and debates related to religion, news, politics, and The New War. Justin Akers is active in antiwar and cross-border solidarity work. He is the author of

"A Draft in the Air? The Just War Tradition, Terrorism and The New War." He said The New War is actually against three enemies: the religious rulers of Iran, the "fascists" of Iraq and Syria, and Islamic extremists like Al Qaeda.

Being Right is The New War… on Freedom.

The New War is the web of crime that threatens America's news, analysis, commentary, interactives, photos, video, audio and web resources. If you're the editor of a [dot]org and a columnist for FoxNews[dot] com, there is only one scenario for American success in Iraq—and it won't be easy. Read first-hand accounts by journalists covering the war in Afghanistan. The world is a free, open, video-streaming website that provides on-demand video of The New War as well as live feeds of social drinking—Balko, Balko, Cato, Radley… Boo.

The New War… on Freedom.

Moved into the sidebar now, Reflections on the American Occupation—It's time for the navigation home, time to pack it in, draw up a synopsis, thank the Cast & Crew, kick back and write a novel about the whole thing, maybe do a couple radio broadcasts. Security will come in the form of books about John Kerry by John Kerry. Unfortunately, the world keeps coming up with things for The New War, like Terror, Technology and Culture, for, um… example.

The New War… on immigrants.

Preventing The New War on Social Drinking, part of our Special Coverage will be taken in moderation, including an hourlong documentary examining the home market for Wargames, Predictions, Military Discussions, Military Jokes and The New War. Special Report: The New War in the Middle East is The New War in the Middle East is The New War, a powerful warning that global crime is robbing us not only of our most important goals in The New War, but also of keeping our sights set on the globe.

The New War… on Poverty. The New War… on poverty.

The back door to international terrorism is ineffective and counterproductive when implemented incrementally—one, two, three, four, five, six, seven… ah, ha, ha… eight, nine, ten years after the September 11 terror attacks. With the steady erosion of our basic rights, we're in danger of becoming driven by people's interests and their seedy well-being and by putting an end to poverty "as we know it."

The New War… on The Poor.

Covering The New War in the weeks since the death of America, a haunting rumor running totally amok about how much money has been spent in the current year arose out of a deluge of Revisionist materials from the Institute for Historical Revision.

A Tragedy of Pearls. On April 25, 1898 the United States declared war on Spain following the sinking of the Battleship Maine in Havana harbor on February 15, 1898.

## The New Way of Life

## The New West

## The New Work(s)

## The New World

## The New Writing

## The New Writing on the Wall

Mark your calendar, dazzle your friends! See the Magic of Global Inequality rising as it's accepted that forgiveness is The New Writing on The Wall.

The question of Time entered the discussion of Post-Graffiti Art in the exhibition at the Swiss Embassy, concluding that forgiveness is The New Writing on the Wall. Nearly all the once-notorious names in Philadelphia graffiti were there, cleverly saying, "This Now is The New Writing on the Wall."

Now, The New Writing on the Wall starts with an author, a topic and a quote.

Now, The New Writing on the Wall has been read 5 times.

The New Writing on the Wall will magically generate its own lexicon.

Singing The New Song to The Web Console Bathroom Vanity, an excellent piece of furniture, can be interpreted as The New Writing on the Wall for bathroom ambience. "1,000 songs in your pocket" is The New Writing on the Wall instead of a clueless quantum note. The New Writing on the Wall is graffiti: But is it better on Concrete or Wallpaper? The students at South Dakota School of Mines & Technology remove graffiti from The New Writing on the Wall. Go inside and look at The New Writing on the Wall. Oh my! Who would write this? Go east on Sanders St. and on the south corner are 2 boxes of shotguns.

97

Forgiveness is The New Writing on the Wall, even as Global Inequality is rising.

Hate Factories are reveling in The New Writing on the Wall, we shouldn't let a bunch of has-beens sabotage a long-delayed future. Now and then, the surviving partners can read The New Writing on the Wall: another way of saying electronic games are here to stay.

Forgiveness is The New Writing on the Wall, the smart way to move through the world.

The New Writing on the Wall is The New Slogan and it's far more informative than it was before—that skeleton will lie in chamber forever.

95

The New Writing on the Wall says: Collaborators wanted. Labor woes continue.

## The New X

## The New XXX

## The New Year's Resolution

## The New You

## The New Zed

# Index

Poems from this book have appeared in the following publications:

*You've Probably Read This Before: An Alumni Anthology from CalArts' MFA Writing Program* (2009): "The New Concrete Poem," "The New Love," "The New Pantoum," "The New Quatrain" and "The New Unrequited Love."

*The Physical Poets Volume 2: "Les Deux"* (Lil' Norton Home Library, 2008): "The New Aesthetic Statement," "The New Birds," "The New New York School," "The New Physicality" and "The New Sky."

*Shampoo 32* (2008): "The New Writing on the Wall."

*A Sing Economy, Flim Forum Volume 2* (2007): "The New Acrostic," "The New Caesura," "The New Concrete Poem," "The New Egret,"The New Emotion," "The New I," "The New Love," "The New Media State," "The New New Deal," "The New Night," "The New Pantoum," "The New Pattern Poem," "The New Quatrain," "The New Rejection Letter," "The New Sapphic," "The New Sprung Rhythm," "The New Subjectivity," "The New Unrequited Love," "The New Villanelle" and "The New War."

$$(p+r)^n$$

**Mathew Timmons** is General Director of General Projects in Los Angeles. His works include *CREDIT* (Blanc Press) and *Lip Service* (Slack Buddha Press).

**Rodrigo Toscano** is the author of *To Leveling Swerve*, *Platform*, *The Disparities*, and *Partisans*. His newest book, *Collapsible Poetics Theater* was a National Poetry Series 2007 winner.

Vincent Dachy acts as the spokesperson of **VD collective** (vdachy@talktalk.net) and has had some *Tribulations* published by Les Figues Press.

ƒ

**LES FIGUES PRESS**
Post Office Box 7736
Los Angeles, CA 90007
www.lesfigues.com